Budgeting

Budgeting

Budgeting

Alan Banks

Grafton College of TAFE

The McGraw-Hill Companies, Inc.

Beijing Bogotà Boston Burr Ridge IL Caracas
Dubuque IA Lisbon London Madison WI
Madrid Mexico City Milan Montreal New Delhi
New York San Francisco Santiago Seoul
Singapore St Louis Sydney Taipei Toronto

Irwin/McGraw-Hill

A Division of The **McGraw·Hill** Companies

Reprinted 1999, 2000, 2002

Text © 1997 McGraw-Hill Book Company Australia Pty Limited
Illustrations and design © 1997 McGraw-Hill Book Company Australia Pty Limited
Additional owners of copyright material are credited on the Acknowledgments page.

National Library of Australia Cataloguing-in-Publication data:

Banks, Alan, 1946– .
Budgeting.

(Includes index.)
ISBN 0 07 470430 3.

1. Budget. I. Title.

658.154

Published in Australia by
McGraw-Hill Book Company Australia Pty Limited
4 Barcoo Street, Roseville NSW 2069, Australia
Publishing Manager: Jae Chung
Editor: Elizabeth Watson
Production management: Elizabeth Watson/Christina Hill
Designer: Jan Schmoeger/Designpoint
Typeset in 10/12 pt Trump Mediaeval
Typeset by Designpoint
Printed by McPherson's Printing Group

Contents

Acknowledgments

The author and publishers acknowledge the permission of the New South Wales Technical and Further Education Commission (NSW TAFE) to include in the text extracts from past NSW TAFE examination papers. Copyright of all NSW TAFE examination papers is held by the NSW TAFE Commission.

For their helpful comments on the manuscript, the author and publishers would also like to thank: Sonia Battistutta, Victoria University of Technology, Victoria; Inal Duman, North Point Institute of TAFE, Queensland; Vaithilintan Elalingam, South Western Sydney Institute of TAFE, NSW; Neville Eley, Launceston Institute of TAFE, Tasmania; John Hamilton, ex-Sydney Institute of Technology, NSW; Ray Jopling, Casey Institute of TAFE, Victoria; and Max Newton, Holmesglen College of TAFE, Victoria.

The staff at McGraw-Hill deserve commendation for their efforts. Special mention must be made of Jae Chung, Publishing Manager, who showed faith in me for this project. My thanks also to Christina Hill, Catherine Dunk and Elizabeth Watson for their support and contributions during the production phase.

This book would not have been completed without the cooperation and support of my wife and daughter. Special thanks go to Pat and Karen Banks.

Preface

Competency-based training and flexible delivery have become the key conceptual tools for education in the Australian TAFE system. The National Accounting Project (NAP) has developed subject modules, in competency based format, for delivery in TAFE accounting courses throughout Australia.

In response to this trend this book has been specifically written for the module *Budgeting* (NAP730) in the TAFE national framework of accounting courses. It is also suitable for any courses containing a basic budgeting unit.

Rarely is the topic of budgeting dealt with in depth in a separate book. Usually it receives brief treatment in one or two chapters in books on financial management and cost or management accounting.

In this text each topic is dissected into easily digestible parts. Each of these parts is followed by a self-test problem which allows for practice and assesses the student's knowledge in a non-threatening way. Immediate feedback is obtained, thus the learner can take appropriate remedial action.

The structure of this book

Each chapter has the following features:

- clearly enunciated learning objectives
- simple explanations enhanced by examples
- a building block approach — new material builds on the material already covered in the chapter or earlier in the book
- self-test problems at strategic points — solutions to each self-test problem are provided at the end of the book and should be used for evaluation after the student has attempted the problem
- end of chapter checklists of important parts of the chapter
- end of chapter questions provided for practice and assessment.

An instructor's resource manual will be available for teachers. The manual will include solutions to chapter questions; masters for overhead transparencies; and additional questions, suitable for assessment tasks (including supervised examinations), as well as their solutions.

Although this book has been designed as a self-paced learning tool it can be equally well used in the normal face-to-face classroom situation.

Cross-referencing grid to *Budgeting* (NAP730)

No.	Assessment criteria	Banks Chapter and page number	Topic
1.1	Define budgeting, and its role in any organisation	1, page 1 1, page 4	What is a budget? Purposes of budgets
1.2	Explain the benefits of budgeting	1, page 6	Benefits and limitations of budgeting
1.3	Define static and flexible budgeting, and continuous budgeting	1, page 7 1, page 7 1, page 8	Static budget Flexible budget Rolling budgets
1.4	List the types of budgets commonly prepared in organisations, which make up a master budget	1, page 9 1, page 11	Master budget Types of budgets
2.1	Prepare the following operating and financial budget schedules, using static budget techniques, for service and trading operations such as service providers (professionals, tradespersons, restaurants, etc), retailers, wholesalers, community or sporting organisations etc:		
	• revenue/sales/fees	2	Revenue budgets for service organisations
	• operating expenses	3	Operating budgets for service organisations
	• income statements	3, page 46 5, page 88	Budgeted revenue statements
	• cash (including collections from accounts receivable)	4 5, page 101	Cash budgets for service organisations Budgeted statements of cash flows
	• balance sheets	5, page 99	Budgeted balance sheets

No.	Assessment criteria	Banks	
		Chapter and page number	Topic
2.2	Prepare the following operating and financial budget schedules, using static budgeting techniques, for a simple manufacturing operation (that is, making one product; one raw material only; factory overhead relating to the factory as a whole, not departmentally; no variances included):	6	Master budgets for manufacturing organisations
	• sales • production • materials purchase and usage • direct labour • factory overhead • cost of goods sold • expenses • income statement • cash (including collections from accounts receivable) • balance sheet		
3.1	Prepare in a flexible budget format, a budgeted income statement for:	8	Flexible budgets
	• a service operation • a trading operation • a manufacturing operation		
4.1	Prepare two different performance reports (based on the types of budgets listed in Learning Outcome 2), which clearly indicate the variance between budget and actual results	7	Performance reports

Chapter 1

Budgeting fundamentals

Objectives

By the end of this chapter you will be able to:

What is a budget?

A **budget** is a formal written statement of management's plans for the future expressed in financial terms.

Budgeting is the process used to develop an organisation's budgets. It is an integral part of planning.

Enlightened Epicures produces gourmet smoked foods for elite Australian restaurants. The organisation has long term plans, medium range plans and short term plans.

- **Long term plans** generally deal with five to ten years into the future, although it is interesting to note that some Japanese companies have a hundred years plan. Long term plans are strategic in nature and are expressed in general terms.
- **Medium range plans** usually span one to five years.

- **Short term plans** range up to one year. These plans are quite detailed and deal with the day to day operations of the business.

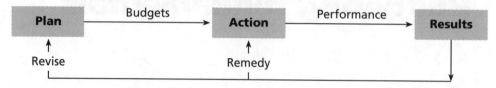

Comparison of actual results to budget

Figure 1.1

Figure 1.1 illustrates the planning cycle. Note that:

- plans, including budgets, are prepared
- action is taken to implement the plans
- performance is measured by comparing actual results to budget
- remedial action is taken, if necessary, or plans are reviewed and reassessed.

Budget preparation

Budgets are plans expressed in financial terms. They are an aid to coordination and control.

It is important that all relevant factors are considered when preparing budgets. Some of these factors are:

- past sales levels and trends
- economic trends
- likely action of competitors
- market research studies
- possible government actions, for example, new legislation affecting the business.

Clarenza Home Building Products manufactures bricks and tiles. Clarenza's Brisbane branch is required to prepare its budgets for the coming year. These budgets will be presented to head office for approval.

To illustrate budget preparation, Brisbane's Administration department will be used. Administration's actual figures for the last financial year were:

	$
Salaries	231 000
Stationery	10 000
Telephone	10 800
Electricity	11 320
Rates	5 555
Depreciation	9 000
	277 675

After carefully considering relevant factors it was estimated that the following changes are likely to occur for the next financial year:

- salaries are expected to increase by 5% — budget will be $231\,000 \times 1.05 = \$242\,550$
- due to a new on-line facility installed by Clarenza, stationery is expected to decrease by 10% — budget will be $\$10\,000 \times 0.9 = \$9000$
- tariff increases will mean that electricity will rise by 6% — budget will be $\$11\,320 \times 1.06 = \$11\,999$, say $12\,000$
- rate increases will be 8% — budget will be $\$5555 \times 1.08 = \$5999.40$, say 6000
- telephone and depreciation should remain the same.

The budget for Administration appears below:

Brisbane Branch: Administration department

Budget for the year ended 30 June

	$
Salaries	242 550
Stationery	9 000
Telephone	10 800
Electricity	12 000
Rates	6 000
Depreciation	9 000
	289 350

Self-test problem 1.1

The Personnel Department of Lanitza Holdings' Farm Machinery Division had the following actual results for last year:

	$
Salaries	154 000
Stationery	3 520
Telephone	7 000
Electricity	7 680
Office Rent	18 000
Depreciation	6 000
	196 200

It is estimated that next year's budget will reflect the following changes:

- salaries to increase by 5%
- stationery to increase by 3%
- telephone usage is expected to decline by 4%
- electricity to increase by 2%

- due to a long term lease, office rent should remain the same
- depreciation — it is anticipated that furniture costing $4000 will be disposed of at the beginning of the financial year and immediately replaced with new furniture costing $5000; the rate of depreciation for furniture is 10% per annum on cost.

Required
Prepare next year's budget for Lanitza Holdings' Farm Machinery Division.

You should now be able to do Question 1.1

Purposes of budgets

The use of budgets is vital if the organisation is to correctly perform necessary management functions. Budgets aid in the planning process. When employed appropriately they facilitate communication and can act as a motivational tool. They are also used as a basis for control and performance measurement.

Planning

Planning necessitates the selection of goals and the establishment of those actions needed to attain the goals. Budgeting forces people in the organisation to plan. Preparation of the budget for the administration department of Clarenza Home Building Products' Brisbane branch means that the administration manager must plan for the staffing and other resources needed to adequately perform administrative functions.

Organising

Organising involves the acquisition and allocation of resources so that the goals of the organisation are efficiently achieved. This includes the arrangement and allocation of work between employees.

Budgets aid the coordination of activities by ensuring different parts of the organisation are working towards the same objectives. For example, the production department will manufacture sufficient quantities to satisfy the demand required by the sales department.

Leading

Leading is primarily aimed at getting organisational members to perform their required tasks in a manner which will help to achieve the organisation's goals. Two important aspects of leading are communicating and motivating.

- **Communicating:** Budgets help communicate to all levels of the business what the organisation's objectives are and how they are to be achieved. Where staff members are allowed to participate in the budget process all parties are more aware of requirements. Budgets also authorise actions to be taken and advise permissible limits, for example, ceilings for expenditure.

- **Motivating:** Budgets provide a target at which group members can aim. They provide a focus for each individual's efforts. When participation is allowed during budget setting those involved in the discussion are more receptive to the decisions made and are more likely to cooperate in achieving the budget.

Controlling

Controlling is the process of setting standards; measuring current performance and comparing it against the standards; and, where necessary, taking remedial action.

It is normal for an organisation to compare actual results with budgets by preparing performance reports. Performance reports are discussed in Chapter 7.

A simple performance report for Trendy Fashions follows:

Trendy Fashions

Performance report for the month of November

	Budget $	Actual $	Variance $	
Sales	50 000	48 000	2 000	U
less Cost of goods sold	30 000	29 500	500	F
Gross profit	20 000	18 500	1 500	U
Marketing expenses	7 500	7 000	500	F
Administration expenses	6 000	6 100	100	U
Financial expenses	1 500	1 500	–	
Operating expenses	15 000	14 600	400	F
Net profit	5 000	3 900	1 100	U

A variance is the difference between budget and actual. Variances are identified as *F* for **favourable** or *U* for **unfavourable**. Note that actual marketing expenses were $500 less than budget and thus the variance was favourable. However, the actual sales were $2000 less than budget, giving an unfavourable variance.

Not all variances will require corrective action. Some variances may be considered immaterial. Others may occur because of faulty budgeting or a change in circumstances, both of which require an amended or new budget.

Self-test problem 1.2

Big 'n Beefy Butchery in Jerramungup WA provides you with the following figures for May:

	Budget $	Actual $
Sales	40 000	41 500
Cost of goods sold	25 000	24 000
Marketing expenses	1 000	1 200
Administration expenses	750	850
Financial expenses	500	450

Required
Prepare a performance report for May.

You should now be able to do Question 1.2

Benefits and limitations of budgeting

Roberts and Irvine[1] identify the following benefits of budgeting:

- It compels management to plan ahead and anticipate the future in a regular and systematic manner.
- It provides all levels of the business with realistic performance targets (business expectations) against which the actual results will be compared.
- It coordinates the segments of a business, making staff aware of how each segment fits together.
- It provides an effective communication tool. Managers exchange information on ideas, business goals and individual achievements.
- If the budgeting process involves staff and contains realistic performance targets it can act as a motivating tool. Management and staff will use the targets as a stimulant to maintain their work effort.

Despite these considerable advantages it must be realised that budgeting has some limitations:

- Budgets cannot ensure that the future has been accurately predicted. Budgets are only estimates and not statements of fact.
- Budgets are no substitute for sound management practices.
- Budgets should not be considered as unalterable. If circumstances change, budgets should be amended accordingly, or new budgets prepared.
- Preparation of a budget does not guarantee success. Success will only come from the efforts of management and staff.

Self-test problem 1.3

Identify which of the following statements are true and which are false. A well managed budgetary process:

(a) enables management to predict the future

(b) provides realistic performance targets

(c) demotivates staff

(d) encourages departmental managers to follow their own agenda

(e) coordinates different sections of a business.

You should now be able to do Question 1.3

Classification of budgets

Static budget

A **static budget** is a budget prepared for one level of activity, for example, a particular volume of production or level of sales.

Flexible budget

The Creative Card Company manufactures inexpensive greeting cards which are sold in packs of ten at discount stores. The Creative Card Company has based its budgets on the premise that it will sell 200 000 packs of cards during the year. What happens if only 190 000 packs of cards are sold?

The Creative Card Company's performance reports will show an unfavourable variance for sales and, most likely, favourable variances for some costs. Those managers responsible for cost control will, no doubt, feel pleased with themselves. Are these self-congratulations justified? After all, the costs at a sales level of 190 000 packs should be lower than at 200 000 packs. Is it possible to make a more realistic comparison? Yes. The Creative Card Company can prepare a flexible budget.

A **flexible budget** is, in fact, several budgets covering a range of activity within which the organisation may operate. The Creative Card Company may prepare its flexible budget at sales levels of 180 000, 190 000, 200 000, 210 000 and 220 000 packs of cards. Flexible budgets are dealt with in Chapter 8.

Before preparing flexible budgets an organisation must first identify its fixed and variable expenses. Study Figure 1.2.

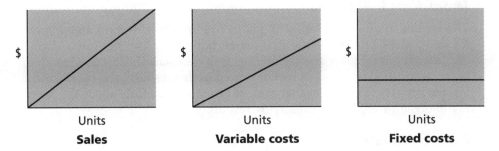

Units	Units	Units
Sales	**Variable costs**	**Fixed costs**

Figure 1.2 *Cost/volume relationships for The Creative Card Company*

Note that as sales increase so do variable costs. However, within the relevant range, fixed costs do not change.

Fixed costs

These are costs which *in total* will tend to remain the same for a period of time and over a particular range of activity. The activity for The Creative Card Company is the number of packs of cards sold. For other organisations it may be volume of production or some other measure.

Fixed costs will not remain at the same dollar value indefinitely. Inflation will cause costs to rise but the increase will not be due to a change in the level of activity.

Examples of fixed costs are rent, rates, building insurance and depreciation.

Variable costs

These are costs which *in total* will tend to increase as the level of activity increases.

Examples of variable costs are electricity, sales commissions, royalties paid to an author, and materials used to manufacture a product.

Self-test problem 1.4

Classify the following as fixed or variable costs:

(a) excess water rates
(b) council rates
(c) fuel oil for factory boiler
(d) salesperson's commission
(e) accountant's salary
(f) lubricants for machinery.

You should now be able to do Questions 1.4 and 1.5

Zero-based budgeting

The normal approach to budgeting is to use historical figures and adjust these for anticipated future events. **Zero-based budgeting** sets the initial figures for each activity to zero. To receive funding from the budgeting process, each activity must be justified in terms of its continued usefulness and the resources needed for that activity. This forces management to think carefully about the operations of the organisation before allocating resources.

Period budgets

Budgets are usually developed for a specified period of time. Short range budgets cover a month, a quarter or a year.

Rolling budgets

The Creative Card Company prepares a cash budget which estimates receipts and payments week by week for thirteen weeks and then month by month for a further twelve months. After the first three months the old weekly budget is dropped off, the first three of the monthly budgets are revised to thirteen weekly budgets and three new months are added to the total period, so that fifteen months of cash receipts and payments are still projected for the future.

Rolling budgets are continually updated by periodically adding a new incremental time period and dropping the period just completed. Rolling budgets are also known as *continuous budgets*.

You should now be able to do Question 1.6

Master budgets

A **master budget** is a combination of all the budgets of an organisation, dealing with all phases of the operations of the business for a particular period of time.

Master budget for a merchandising firm

A merchandising firm is a business that buys and sells goods — wholesalers and retailers. Figure 1.3 depicts a typical master budget for a merchandising firm.

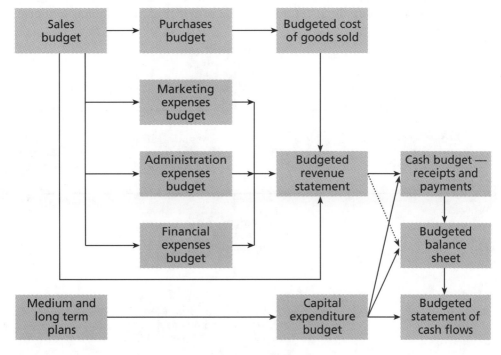

Figure 1.3 *Master budget for a merchandising firm*

Although an attempt has been made to show relationships between budgets with the use of arrows it should be noted that all budgets are interrelated and impact on each other. Normally the starting point for the preparation of the master budget is the sales or revenue budget. Other budgets are then prepared to reflect the required income.

It is appropriate to distinguish cash budgets from budgeted statements of cash flows. A **cash budget** shows the estimated cash receipts and payments and the estimated bank balance for a given period or periods.

Accounting standards AAS 28 and AASB 1026, both entitled *Statement of Cash Flows*, require businesses to prepare a statement, in a designated format, containing information about the business's cash flows during the reporting period. A **budgeted statement of cash flows** is the predicted cash flows for a future period presented in this required format.

As capital expenditure budgets are beyond the scope of this book they are dealt with briefly here and not mentioned again. All other budgets are discussed and illustrated throughout the text.

The **capital expenditure budget** quantifies the capital investment decisions determined in the organisation's long term plans.

Master budget for a provider of professional services

Merchandising firms form one segment of service industries. The provision of professional services represents another segment. Accountants, lawyers, doctors, educational institutions and others all need to prepare budgets. Figure 1.4 represents a simplified master budget for a provider of professional services.

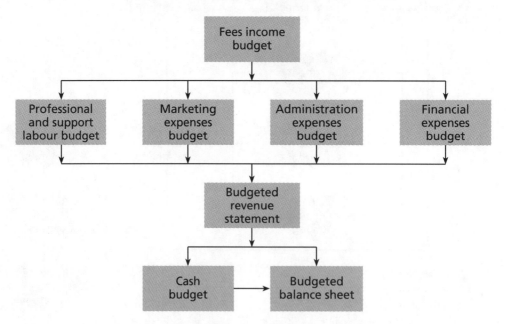

Figure 1.4 *Simplified master budget for a provider of professional services*

The major difference between Figures 1.3 and 1.4 is that the sales budget has been replaced by a fees income budget. The cost of goods sold budget has disappeared as no goods are being sold. A new professional and support labour budget appears because the business is 'selling' professional expertise and knowledge.

Master budget for a manufacturing organisation

Manufacturing organisations are those businesses which make a tangible product, for example, televisions, motor cars, tennis racquets. Budgets for manufacturing organisations are illustrated in Chapter 6. Figure 1.5 illustrates the components of a master budget for a manufacturing organisation.

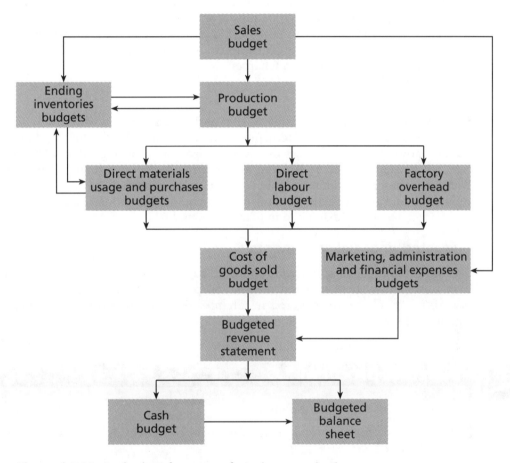

Figure 1.5 *Master budget for a manufacturing organisation*

You should now be able to do Questions 1.7 and 1.8

Types of budgets

Budgets are traditionally categorised as revenue budgets, operating budgets and budgeted financial statements.

Revenue budgets

Revenue budgets are estimates of the income of an organisation for a specific period.

It has already been noted that preparation of revenue budgets form the beginning of the budgeting process. Consider The Creative Card Company — it needs to estimate the number of packs of cards it will sell so that it knows how many to produce. This, in turn, dictates what materials are needed, how many employees (with what skills) are required, and so on.

It is apparent that revenue forecasting is a critical step in the budgeting process. Revenue budgets for service organisations are illustrated in Chapter 2 and for manufacturing organisations in Chapter 6.

Operating budgets

Operating budgets are those budgets that estimate activities which will affect profit. Examples for a manufacturing organisation are the production budget, direct materials budget, factory overhead budget and cost of goods sold budget.

Cash budgets can be considered as operating budgets or financial budgets. Because of their importance they are dealt with separately in Chapter 4 for service industries and included in Chapter 6 for manufacturing organisations. Other operating budgets are discussed in Chapters 3 and 6.

Budgeted financial statements

The budgeted revenue statement, budgeted balance and budgeted statement of cash flows show the estimated results and projected financial position of an organisation. These are covered in Chapter 5 for service organisations and Chapter 6 for manufacturing organisations.

Self-test problem 1.5

Select the most suitable response.

1 A budget that is prepared for one level of activity is which one of the following?

(a) Rolling budget
(b) Continuous budget
(c) Operating budget
(d) Static budget

2 A budget that estimates activities that will affect profit is which one of the following?

(a) Rolling budget
(b) Operating budget
(c) Budgeted financial statement
(d) Static budget

3 A budget that covers a range of activities within which an organisation may operate is which one of the following?

    (a) Static budget
    (b) Rolling budget
    (c) Flexible budget
    (d) Master budget

4 A budget that is continuously updated by adding a new incremental period and dropping off the period just completed is which one of the following?

    (a) Rolling budget
    (b) Period budget
    (c) Operating budget
    (d) Master budget

5 Which pair of the following terms are synonymous?

    (a) Rolling budgets, continuous budgets
    (b) Static budgets, flexible budgets
    (c) Period budgets, rolling budgets
    (d) Master budgets, zero-based budgets

You should now be able to do Question 1.9

Behavioural aspects of budgeting

How budgets are administered impacts on their effectiveness in helping to achieve an organisation's goals. 'The budget in any company has a dual role of being a forecast of the year and a yardstick of managerial performance.'[2]

It can also be argued that by using the budget to measure managerial performance there is an attempt to use it as a tool for control. If this is linked with a reward and/or punishment system: 'There is a general tendency for managers to distort the information they pass on to their superiors, so that the unfavourable items are under-emphasised.'[3]

Such distortion of information is undesirable and counter-productive.

Some organisations use sanctions and punishments to encourage adherence to budget. The use of sanctions and punishment is synonymous with an authoritarian style of management. Typical responses to this use of budgets are:

- *manager's comment:* 'The important thing for us to do is to follow up. The supervisor's interest lags unless someone is constantly checking up on him … I think there is a need for more pressure … I think that man is inherently lazy and if we could only increase the pressure budgets would be more effective.'[4]
- *supervisor:* 'You got to outwit that son-of-a-bitch … Remember the bastards are out to screw you, and that's all they got to think about.'[5]

The use of sanctions and punishment are more likely to lead to resentment and further attempts to beat the system. At best it will result in a defeated and less than enthusiastic employee. It will certainly encourage behaviour such as 'padding the budget'.

Padding the budget

Bill Smithers is the manager of the Administration Department at Clarenza Building Products' Brisbane branch. Bill is responsible for ensuring that costs for the Administration Department do not exceed budget. Knowing this Bill always submits estimates to the budget committee that exceed what he believes the true costs will be.

Margaret White is the manager of the Sales Department at Brisbane branch. Margaret submits a conservative estimate for sales knowing that if the branch's sales exceed budget she will appear in a favourable light to senior management.

These are examples of padding the budget. **Padding the budget** means over estimating costs and/or under estimating revenue. The difference between the padded estimate and a realistic estimate is known as **budgetary slack**. For example, if Bill Smithers believes that a realistic estimate for administrative salaries for the year is $160 000 but submits $180 000 to the budget committee he has built $20 000 slack into the budget.

An additional reason why managers pad the budget is that in many organisations the submitted estimate is changed by the resource allocation authority. That is, budgeted costs are reduced and budgeted revenues increased.

Participation in the budgetary process

Hopwood reports on a series of experiments conducted by Bass and Leavitt. Managers were given two plans, one developed by themselves and the other created for them. Half of the managers operated their own plan first and half operated their own plan second. 'The results of the experiment showed that the managers were both more productive and more satisfied with their job and their colleagues when operating their own plans … they had a greater commitment to making them work.'[6]

It was also found that less time was wasted on competition between the planners and doers when the managers implemented their own plans.

While not advocating that lower level managers be given carte blanche to set their own plan it is suggested that they should be included in the budget setting process and their opinions be sought and carefully considered.

Advantages arising from participation are:

- improved communication
- greater understanding of the factors involved
- problems can be thrashed out at budget meetings before the budget is set
- increased acceptance of budget
- improved commitment
- by utilising the manager's expertise there is a real likelihood of an improvement in the quality of the budget itself.

Argyris[7] suggests that participation may help ease the pressure and tension created by budgets.

He also makes the point that if top management is going to use participation it should be used in the true sense of the word. Any watering down or pretence will lead to distrust and suspicion by subordinates.

Other factors affecting behaviour

Some budgetary problems which may cause dysfunctional behaviour are:

- budget targets which are perceived by employees as too difficult to attain will result in resentment and a feeling of stress
- budget targets which are perceived by staff as too easy to achieve do not provide a challenge and may lead to a slipshod performance by staff
- management may feel a loss of autonomy by feeling that they are hemmed in by the budget and do not have sufficient flexibility to use their own initiative
- managers may become narrow minded, focusing only on their own department, resulting in disadvantage to the organisation as a whole
- the emphasis on financial goals to the detriment of non-financial goals may have a debilitating effect on the organisation.

Non-financial measures of performance

Horngren and Foster[8] advise that variances should be used for attention directing, not as problem solvers. That is, they indicate areas which require further investigation, not that the manager involved is seen as a problem that needs fixing.

To overcome a reliance on financial measures for performance evaluation Horngren and Foster go on to suggest that non-financial measures should be considered. They give two examples: 'first-time through yield — the percentage of products manufactured "right" (to specification) the first time, and throughput time — the time that a product takes from the first stage of manufacture to completion.'[9]

Finally, they suggest that many companies use a combination of both financial and non-financial measures when evaluating the performance of their managers. The latter makes sense considering that there are many factors, for example, personal problems, reliance on other departments, which are not directly measurable in dollar terms.

You should now be able to do Questions 1.10 and 1.11

Checklist

Before progressing to the next chapter, complete the checklist below. This will identify whether you have an understanding of the important parts of the chapter.

Can you do the following?

- ☐ Define budgeting
- ☐ Explain the roles of budgets
- ☐ List the benefits and limitations of budgeting
- ☐ Define static and flexible budgeting
- ☐ Explain the different types of budgets
- ☐ Discuss behavioural aspects of budgeting

Questions

1.1 Explain budgeting.

1.2 (a) Explain how a budget facilitates communication and coordination.

(b) How do budgets assist management to carry out the control function?

1.3 List three benefits and three limitations of budgeting.

1.4 Classify the following costs as fixed or variable:

(a) annual factory lease

(b) salesperson's commission

(c) cocoa used in chocolate manufacture

(d) credit manager's salary

(e) flour used in baking bread

(f) insurance on factory premises

(g) repairs and maintenance to motor vehicles.

1.5 Define each of the following terms:

(a) static budget

(b) flexible budget

(c) fixed expenses

(d) variable expenses.

1.6 Explain:

(a) zero-based budgeting

(b) period budgets

(c) rolling budgets.

1.7 What is a master budget?

1.8 (a) List five budgets which would be included in a master budget for a merchandising firm.

(b) List two budgets for a supplier of professional services which would not be found in the master budget of a merchandising firm.

(c) Nominate one budget which would be prepared for a manufacturing organisation but not for a business in the service industry.

1.9 Briefly explain:

(a) revenue budgets

(b) operating budgets

(c) budgeted financial statements.

1.10 Define the term budgetary slack and briefly describe a problem it can cause.[10]

1.11 Why is participative budgeting often an effective tool?[11]

Endnotes

1 Roberts, S. and Irvine, J., *Financial Accounting A CBT Approach*, Sydney, Aust: McGraw-Hill Book Company, 1996, p. 6
2 Schiff, M. and Lewin, A. Y., 'Where Traditional Budgeting Fails' in DeCoster, D. T., Ramanathan, K. V. and Sundem, G. L. (eds), *Accounting for Managerial Decision Making*, 2nd edn, New York, USA: John Wiley & Sons, 1978, p. 349
3 Lamberton, G. and Harvey, D., *Advanced Management Accounting*, Course Notes, East Lismore, NSW: Southern Cross University, 1991
4 Hopwood, A., *Accounting and Human Behaviour*, London, England: Haymarket Publishing Ltd, 1974, p. 66
5 Hopwood, p. 6
6 Hopwood, p. 75
7 Argyris, G., 'Human Problems With Budgeting', *Harvard Business Review*, 31(1), Jan–Feb, 1953, pp. 97–110
8 Horngren, C. T. and Foster, G., *Cost Accounting — A Managerial Emphasis*, 7th edn, Englewood Cliffs, USA: Prentice Hall Inc., 1991
9 Horngren, p. 272
10 Hilton, R., *Managerial Accounting*, 2nd edn, New York, USA: McGraw-Hill Book Company, 1994
11 Hilton

Chapter 2

Revenue budgets for service organisations

Objectives

By the end of this chapter you will be able to:

Introduction

The preparation of revenue budgets involves forecasting future events.

Heizer and Render say: 'Forecasting is the art and science of predicting future events. It may involve taking historical data and projecting them into the future with some sort of mathematical model. It may be a subjective or intuitive prediction of the future. Or it may involve a combination of these, that is mathematical model adjusted by a manager's good judgement.'[1]

Revenue budgets may be prepared by product, by period, for sales areas or a combination of these.

You should now be able to do Question 2.1

Forecasting methods

There are two basic ways to undertake the task of forecasting. **Qualitative methods** rely on a manager's attitudes, beliefs, feelings, experience and intuition.

Quantitative methods use mathematical models based on historical data or causal variables. It is common for businesses to use both methods concurrently.

Qualitative methods

These include:

- **Jury of executive opinion:** A select group of managers are consulted. The group meets and arrives at an estimate of demand.
- **Sales force composite:** Each salesperson submits an estimate of the sales they believe they will achieve during the coming period. District managers review these estimates and forward aggregated district forecasts to regional managers. Regional managers combine the district forecasts and forward the revised regional forecast to head office.
- **The Delphi technique:** This is similar to the jury of executive opinion in that it is a method for combining the opinions of experts. It differs in that the opinions are obtained through questionnaires rather than the participants meeting face to face. This avoids the possibility of personal conflicts and one person unduly influencing others.
- **Market research:** Customers are surveyed in an attempt to find out which products they intend to buy and in what quantities.

Quantitative methods

As qualitative methods are based on opinions they are necessarily subjective. Quantitative methods use mathematical models and are more objective. Quantitative methods can be categorised into two groups.

- **Time series models:** These models take historical data and project into the future. Typical time series models are moving averages, exponential smoothing and trend projection using the least squares method.
- **Causal models:** These models assume that the item being forecast is linked to some other variable. For example, the sale of building products may be predicted from home building approvals. Causal models use linear regression and correlation.

Quantitative methods are dealt with in books on quantitative analysis and statistics.

Self-test problem 2.1

Identify the most correct response to the following:

1 When a select group of managers meet and arrive at an estimate of demand it is known as which of the following?

(a) Jury of executive opinion
(b) Sales force composite
(c) The Delphi technique
(d) Market research

2 When customers and potential customers are asked about their proposed buying behaviour this is which of the following?

(a) Jury of executive opinion
(b) Sales force composite
(c) The Delphi technique
(d) Market research

3 When each salesperson submits an estimate of sales it is known as which of the following?

(a) Jury of executive opinion
(b) Sales force composite
(c) The Delphi technique
(d) Market research

4 When experts' opinions are sought by the use of questionnaires it is called which of the following?

(a) Jury of executive opinion
(b) Sales force composite
(c) The Delphi technique
(d) Market research

You should now be able to do Question 2.2

Factors affecting revenue forecasting

Hilton[2] advises that the major factors to be considered when preparing revenue budgets include:

- past sales levels and trends for the firm developing the forecast as well as for the entire industry
- general economic trends (Is the economy growing? How fast? Is a recession or economic slowdown expected?)
- economic trends in the company's industry (In the petroleum industry, for example, is personal travel likely to increase, thereby implying increased demand for gasoline?)
- other factors expected to affect sales in the industry (Is an unusually cold winter expected, which would result in increased demand for home heating oil in southern climates?)
- political and legal events (Is legislation pending, for example, that would affect the demand for petroleum, such as tax incentives to use alternative energy sources?)
- the intended pricing policy of the company
- planned advertising and product promotion
- expected actions of competitors
- new products contemplated by the company or other firms (Has an automobile firm, for example, announced the development of a new vehicle that runs on battery power, thereby reducing the demand for gasoline?)
- market research studies.

You should now be able to do Question 2.3

Sales budgets

Merchandising and manufacturing firms prepare sales budgets. There is really no difference in the preparation of sales budgets for both types of organisations. Merchandising organisations are illustrated in this chapter and sales budgets are revisited in Chapter 6 for manufacturing organisations.

Sales budgets can be prepared by product, by period, by area or some combination of these.

Sales by product

RAD Designs produces three backpack school bags. Each style of bag is designed for a separate market. Small is for infant school children, medium for primary school children and large for high school students.

Estimated sales volumes for the coming year are 12 000 small, 9600 medium and 8000 large. The estimated sales prices are small $30, medium $35 and large $40. Fiona Williams, the budget accountant, prepared the following sales budget.

RAD Designs

Sales budget for the year ending 30 June

Style of backpack	Sales volume Units	Sales price $	Sales $
Small	12 000	30	360 000
Medium	9 600	35	336 000
Large	8 000	40	320 000
			1 016 000

All Fiona had to do was multiply the estimated price per unit by the estimated sales volume.

Self-test problem 2.2

Halls Hardware is preparing its budgets for the coming year. Its small gardening section sells spades, forks and hoes. Estimated sales volumes for the coming year are 4000 spades, 2500 forks and 2000 hoes. Estimated sales prices are $50, $40 and $30 respectively.

Required
Prepare a sales budget for the Gardening Section of Halls Hardware for the coming year ending 30 June.

You should now be able to do Question 2.4

In the example for RAD Designs the estimated sales volumes and sales prices were provided. To arrive at these figures it is normal practice to take the previous period's figures and adjust for known factors that are likely to affect future sales.

Gourmet Biscuits is a retailer of specialty biscuits sold in one kilogram lots. Gourmet's sales figures for the last financial year are:

Type of biscuit	Sales volume kg	Amount $
Sweet Hearts	50 000	400 000
Cherry Surprises	40 000	280 000
Chocolate Supremes	60 000	360 000
Almond Delights	30 000	150 000
	180 000	1 190 000

It is anticipated that demand for Sweet Hearts will decrease by 10%; Cherry Surprises will increase by 2.5%; Chocolate Supremes will decrease by 5%; and Almond Delights will increase by 7.5%. There will be an across the board price increase of 4%.

Bishen Singh, Gourmet Biscuits' accountant, prepared the following sales budget for the next financial year:

Gourmet Biscuits

Sales budget for the year ending 30 June

Type of biscuit	Sales volume kg	Sales price $	Sales $
Sweet Hearts	45 000	8.30	373 500
Cherry Surprises	41 000	7.30	299 300
Chocolate Supremes	57 000	6.25	356 250
Almond Delights	32 250	5.20	167 700
			1 196 750

Bishen set about preparing the sales budget in the following manner.

Step 1

He found the present sale price per kilogram:

Type of biscuit	
Sweet Hearts	$400 000/50 000 = $8
Cherry Surprises	$280 000/40 000 = $7
Chocolate Supremes	$360 000/60 000 = $6
Almond Delights	$150 000/30 000 = $5

Step 2

Bishen calculated the new prices, keeping in mind the 4% increase:

Type of biscuit

Sweet Hearts	$8 × 1.04 = $8.32 (rounded to $8.30)
Cherry Surprises	$7 × 1.04 = $7.28 (rounded to $7.30)
Chocolate Supremes	$6 × 1.04 = $6.24 (rounded to $6.25)
Almond Delights	$5 × 1.04 = $5.20

Step 3

He computed the estimated sales volume allowing for the anticipated increases and decreases in demand:

Type of biscuit

Sweet Hearts	50 000 × 0.9 = 45 000 kg
Cherry Surprises	40 000 × 1.025 = 41 000 kg
Chocolate Supremes	60 000 × 0.95 = 57 000 kg
Almond Delights	30 000 × 1.075 = 32 250 kg

Step 4

Bishen completed the budget shown earlier by multiplying the estimated sales volumes by the estimated selling prices.

Self-test problem 2.3

Romanesque Fragrances Ltd sells three brands of perfume. Sales figures for the last financial year were:

Type of perfume	Sales volumes Litres	Amount $
Venus	3 600	1 440 000
Romantic Holiday	5 000	1 750 000
Balmy Breezes	8 000	1 600 000
	16 600	4 790 000

For the coming financial year it is proposed to increase the price of Balmy Breezes by 10% and reduce the prices of Venus and Romantic Holiday by 6%. Anticipated demand for Venus is the same as last year; Romantic Holiday should increase by 2%; and Balmy Breezes decrease by 5%.

Required

Prepare the sales budget for the coming financial year.

You should now be able to do Question 2.5

Sales by period

The sales budgets illustrated thus far have all been for one year. It is usual for the yearly budget to be broken down into quarterly or monthly figures.

Clarrie Mathews operates a mobile fast food van which visits the local factories during meal breaks. Clarrie's sales figures for the first quarter of this calendar year are:

	Hot Dogs		Pies		Drinks	
	Units	$	Units	$	Units	$
January	10 500	21 000	12 600	18 900	21 000	23 100
February	10 000	20 000	12 000	18 000	20 000	22 000
March	11 500	23 000	13 800	20 700	23 000	25 300
	32 000	64 000	38 400	57 600	64 000	70 400

Clarrie is preparing a sales budget, month by month, for the first quarter of next year.

Step 1

He calculates the present average price for each product:

Product	
Hot Dogs	$64 000/32 000 = $2
Pies	$57 600/38 400 = $1.50
Drinks	$70 400/64 000 = $1.10

Step 2

Next Clarrie decides to increase all prices by 10%:

Product	
Hot Dogs	$2 × 1.1 = $2.20
Pies	$1.50 × 1.1 = $1.65
Drinks	$1.10 × 1.1 = $1.21 (say $1.20)

Despite the price increase Clarrie believes sales volume will rise by 5% for each item.

Step 3

He calculates the new sales volume as:

	Hot Dogs	Pies	Drinks
January	10 500 × 1.05 = 11 025	12 600 × 1.05 = 13 230	21 000 × 1.05 = 22 050
February	10 000 × 1.05 = 10 500	12 000 × 1.05 = 12 600	20 000 × 1.05 = 21 000
March	11 500 × 1.05 = 12 075	13 800 × 1.05 = 14 490	23 000 × 1.05 = 24 150

Step 4

Clarrie now prepares the budget:

Clarrie's Mobile Smoko

Sales budget for the quarter ending 31 March

	January	February	March	Total for the quarter
Hot Dogs				
Sales volume	11 025	10 500	12 075	33 600
Selling price	$2.20	$2.20	$2.20	$2.20
Sales	$24 255	$23 100	$26 565	$73 920
Pies				
Sales volume	13 230	12 600	14 490	40 320
Selling price	$1.65	$1.65	$1.65	$1.65
Sales	$21 830	$20 790	$23 908	$66 528
Drinks				
Sales volume	22 050	21 000	24 150	67 200
Selling price	$1.20	$1.20	$1.20	$1.20
Sales	$26 460	$25 200	$28 980	$80 640
Total sales	$72 545	$69 090	$79 453	$221 088

Self-test problem 2.4

Electronics Inc. sells two types of solid-state semi-conductor boards, Model SX3 and Model TX5. Electronics Inc.'s estimated sales volumes for the first quarter of the next financial year are:

	July	August	September
Model SX3	150	120	130
Model TX5	160	135	140

Expected selling prices per unit are:

	July $	August $	September $
Model SX3	450	450	465
Model TX5	300	310	310

Required

Prepare a sales budget, month by month, for the quarter ending 30 September.

You should now be able to do Question 2.6

Sales by area

Rebecca Johnson, budget accountant, is preparing the sales budget for Valley View Cordials. Valley View has retail outlets in all states on mainland Australia. It sells the soft drinks in crates of one dozen bottles for $20 per crate. Prices should not change for next year.

After consultation with Stephanie Pullen, marketing manager, Rebecca came up with the following estimates of sales by state by month (in crates) for the quarter ending 31 December:

	Qld	NSW	Vic.	SA	WA
October	9 600	12 120	10 980	8 100	4 200
November	10 740	11 700	10 500	7 680	4 920
December	10 320	13 440	13 260	8 460	3 540

Rebecca's approach to producing the quarterly sales budget by sales area was substantially the same as that illustrated for sales budget by product. Rebecca's final sales budget appears below:

Valley View Cordials

Sales budget for the quarter ending 31 December

	October	November	December	Total for the quarter
Queensland				
Sales volume	9 600	10 740	10 320	30 660
Selling price	$20	$20	$20	$20
Sales	$192 000	$214 800	$206 400	$613 200
New South Wales				
Sales volume	12 120	11 700	13 440	37 260
Selling price	$20	$20	$20	$20
Sales	$242 400	$234 000	$268 800	$745 200
Victoria				
Sales volume	10 980	10 500	13 260	34 740
Selling price	$20	$20	$20	$20
Sales	$219 600	$210 000	$265 200	$694 800
South Australia				
Sales volume	8 100	7 680	8 460	24 240
Selling price	$20	$20	$20	$20
Sales	$162 000	$153 600	$169 200	$484 800
Western Australia				
Sales volume	4 200	4 920	3 540	12 660
Selling price	$20	$20	$20	$20
Sales	$84 000	$98 400	$70 800	$253 200
Total sales	$900 000	$910 800	$980 400	$2 791 200

Self-test problem 2.5

The Mower Specialists operate retail outlets in Ballarat and Bendigo. They sell two types of mowers. Estimated sales prices for the coming quarter are:

	Month 1	Month 2	Month 3
Two stroke	$450	$450	$475
Four stoke	$600	$630	$630

Anticipated sales volumes are:

	Month 1	Month 2	Month 3
Ballarat			
Two stroke	15	18	19
Four stoke	10	12	16
Bendigo			
Two stroke	11	14	14
Four stoke	8	9	12

Required
Prepare a sales budget, month by month, by sales area for the quarter.

You should now be able to do Question 2.7

Fees income budgets

Accountants, lawyers, doctors, educational institutions and other service providers also need to prepare revenue budgets. Many of these organisations base their budgets on estimated hours of work at an estimated hourly rate.

Paul Wimble is a senior partner in the accounting firm of Wimble, Tensby and Associates, located in Tenterfield NSW. Last year the firm charged clients with 10 400 hours. The average hourly rate charged to clients was $90. Market research indicated that Wimble and Tensby had 20% of the market in Tenterfield and this should rise to 22% next year. Paul has decided to increase the hourly rate charged to clients by 4%.

He estimated the fees to be received next year as follows:

- anticipated client hours — increase in market share is 2%, which represents an increase on current market share of (2/20 × 100) 10%, therefore, estimated client hours for next year are (10 400 × 1.1) 11 440
- desired charge out rate — $90 × 1.04 = $93.60.

The fees income budget can now be prepared:

Wimble, Tensby and Associates

Fees income budget for the year ending 30 June

Estimated client hours	11 440
Estimated hourly charge	$93.60
	$1 070 784

Self-test problem 2.6

Manners and Fitzloon is a firm of solicitors. Hours booked to clients last year were 15 000. The charge out rate was $85 per hour. The firm has decided to increase the hourly rate by 8% for the next year. The firm's current market share is 22% and this is anticipated to increase to 25% next year.

Required
Prepare the fees income budget for the coming year ending 30 June.

You should now be able to do Question 2.8

As with merchandising firms, providers of professional services also prepare budgets month by month or quarter by quarter etc.

Carol Dewar is setting up a new naturopath clinic in Burnie, Tasmania. Carol hopes to start seeing patients on 1 July. The only staff she intends to employ is a receptionist/clerk. She has decided to work five days per week and eight hours each day. Carol will take four weeks holidays per year. It is estimated that Carol will work for sixty-five days during the quarter ending 30 September. She believes she will be fully occupied.

Eighty per cent of the time will be taken up by consultations in Carol's rooms, the remainder of her time will be taken up with home visits. Carol estimates home visits will take one hour per patient and half an hour for normal consultations. She is going to charge $60 for home visits and $35 for normal consultations.

Carol wishes to prepare a fees income budget for the first quarter of operations.

- Carol needs to calculate the number of consultations she will be conducting for the quarter. She starts by estimating the number of hours she will be working during the quarter — 65 days × 8 hours = 520 hours.
- The time spent on each type of consultation is computed — home visits 20% × 520 = 104 hours; normal consultations 80% × 520 = 416 hours. As home visits take one hour each Carol will make 104 home visits. As normal consultations take half an hour each she will conduct (416 × 2) 832 normal consultations.
- Now Carol must estimate the consultations for each month. She believes she will work 23 days in July, 22 days in August and 20 days in September. Carol calculates the number of visits for each month as:

	Normal	Home
July	23/65 × 832 = 294	23/65 × 104 = 37
August	22/65 × 832 = 282	22/65 × 104 = 35
September	20/65 × 832 = 256	20/65 × 104 = 32
	832	104

- The final step is to prepare the budget itself:

Carol Dewar

Fees income budget for the quarter ending 30 September

	July	August	September	Total for the quarter
Normal consultations				
Number of patients	294	282	256	832
Consultation fee	$35	$35	$35	$35
Fees income	$10 290	$9 870	$8 960	$29 120
Home visits				
Number of patients	37	35	32	104
Consultation fee	$60	$60	$60	$60
Fees income	$2 220	$2 100	$1 920	$6 240
Total fees income	$12 510	$11 970	$10 880	$35 360

Self-test problem 2.7

Brita Carpet Cleaning Service provides three types of carpet cleaning services. Brita charges $40 per hour. The times taken for each type of cleaning service are:

- super shampoo — 4 hours
- standard shampoo — 3 hours
- quick shampoo — 2 hours.

Brita has six operators who each work 1650 hours per annum — 30% of their time is spent doing super shampoos, 50% on standard shampoos and 20% on quick shampoos.

Required

(a) Prepare an annual fees income budget for the year ending 30 June.
(b) Prepare a fees income budget, month by month and by service, for the quarter ending 30 June. Assume that the proportions of numbers of shampoos per month to the year's totals are: April 8%; May 10%; June 9%.

You should now be able to do Question 2.9

Not all service organisations are strictly merchandising or strictly professional service providers. Many are a combination of both. In addition, many organisations earn other forms of income — for example, income from investments, rental income and commission received.

Carol Dewar not only conducts consultations, she also sells vitamin and mineral supplements and herbal remedies. In addition, she sub-lets one of her rooms and receives interest on investments. A quarterly budget could look like this:

Carol Dewar

Revenue budget for the quarter ending 30 September

	July	August	September	Total for the quarter
	$	$	$	$
Consultation fees				
Normal	10 290	9 870	8 960	29 120
Home visits	2 220	2 100	1 920	6 240
Fees income	12 510	11 970	10 880	35 360
Sales				
Vitamins and minerals	1 750	1 430	1 310	4 490
Herbal remedies	1 450	1 550	1 430	4 430
Sales income	3 200	2 980	2 740	8 920
Other income				
Rental income	500	500	500	1 500
Investment interest			150	150
Total other income	500	500	650	1 650
Total revenue	16 210	15 450	14 270	45 930

You should now be able to do Questions 2.10 to 2.12

Checklist

Before progressing to the next chapter, complete the checklist below. This will identify whether you have an understanding of the important parts of the chapter.

Can you do the following?

- ☐ Explain sales forecasting
- ☐ Identify different forecasting methods
- ☐ List factors which impact on revenue forecasting
- ☐ Prepare sales budgets for merchandising organisations
- ☐ Prepare fees income budgets for providers of professional services

Questions

2.1 Define forecasting.

2.2 Briefly discuss quantitative techniques for forecasting.

2.3 List five factors which should be taken into consideration when forecasting revenue.

2.4 Ball Sports specialise in retailing balls for certain sporting activities. Estimated sale prices for the coming year are rugby balls $25 each, soccer balls $27 each, basketballs $30 each and tennis balls $15 per can. Sales volumes are predicted to be: rugby 10 000; soccer 9000; basketballs 12 000; and tennis balls (cans) 18 000. Prepare a sales budget for the coming year ending 30 June.

2.5 Alzaria Products sells chemicals to manufacturing organisations. The sales figures for the year just ending are:

Product	Sales volume Litres	Amount $
Siluria	100 000	1 000 000
Malus	50 000	350 000
Zyton	80 000	640 000
	230 000	1 990 000

Anticipated variations to sales volumes are: Siluria 8% increase; Malus 4% increase; Zyton 6% decrease. All sales prices will increase by 5%. Prepare the sales budget for the coming year ending 30 June.

2.6 Webster Discounts had the following sales figures for the six months ended 30 June last year:

	$
January	180 000
February	190 000
March	210 000
April	240 000
May	220 000
June	195 000

It is expected that next year there will be an increase in sales volume of 6% and an increase in prices of 4%.

Required

Prepare a sales budget for next year for the six months ending 30 June. Calculations may be rounded to the nearest thousand dollars.

2.7 Sundem Stores has branches in each of the eastern states of Australia. Average sales price was $50. It has been decided to increase prices for the coming year as follows: Tasmania 6%; Victoria 2%; New South Wales 3%; Queensland 5%. Sales volumes for the first quarter of last year were:

	Tas.	Vic.	NSW	Qld
January	3 500	9 100	8 000	6 700
February	4 100	8 700	8 900	6 400
March	2 900	11 000	8 600	7 000

It is anticipated that sales volumes for the coming year will vary from last year: Tasmania 5% decrease; New South Wales 4% increase; Queensland 2% decrease. There will be no change for Victoria.

Required

Prepare a sales budget, month by month and by state, for the quarter ending 31 March.

2.8 Bridge Street Medical Centre has asked you to prepare its fees income budget for next year. Fees for this year were $3 000 000. This represented 20% of the market. By reducing fees by 5% it is thought that the centre's market share should increase to 24% next year. The total market is also expected to increase by 4% next year. Calculate the fees income that the Bridge Street Medical Centre can expect to receive next year.

2.9 St Jude's Musical Academy conducts music lessons. The rate charged per lesson last year was: guitar $27; piano $29; woodwind and brass $31. It is proposed to increase all fees by $3 per lesson for the coming year. The number of lessons given during the quarter ended 30 September last year were:

	July	August	September
Guitar	160	150	170
Piano	180	160	160
Woodwind and brass	60	50	65

For the coming year St Jude's anticipates a 5% increase in guitar lessons, no change for piano, and a 2% increase in woodwind and brass lessons.

Required

Prepare a fees income budget, month by month and by type of lesson, for the quarter ending 30 September of the coming year. Round calculations to the nearest whole number.

REVENUE BUDGETS FOR SERVICE ORGANISATIONS • **33**

2.10 Healthworks Inc. is a physical therapy and sports medicine practice in Darwin. Healthworks provides you with the following projected figures:

	1st quarter	2nd quarter	3rd quarter	4th quarter
Professional services: office visits	1 940	2 000	1 920	1 960
Sale of orthotic devices	150	180	120	160

Healthworks charge an average $45 per visit and the average selling price of orthotic devices is $90 per device.

Required

Prepare a revenue budget, by quarter, for the year ending 30 June.[3]

2.11 Yellow Jersey Bikes sells two different types of bicycles. One is a racing bike which sells for $500 and the other is a mountain bike which sells for $600. Budgeted sales for the quarter ending 31 March are shown below:

	Racing	Mountain
January	63	38
February	67	43
March	72	46

Required

Prepare a sales budget, month by month, by product for the quarter ending 31 March.

2.12 Mawdryn Enterprises provides you with the following information:
- actual sales last year:

Product	Units	Price per Unit
A	18 000	$7.50
B	30 000	$2.50
C	15 000	$5

- estimated changes in demand for the coming year:

Product A	12% increase
Product B	6% decrease
Product C	10% increase

- estimated product sales per quarter expressed as a percentage of total annual sales:

Product	Jan–Mar	Apr–June	July–Sept	Oct–Dec
A	25	30	25	20
B	20	25	25	30
C	25	15	30	30

- all prices will be increased by 6% for the coming year.

Required

Prepare a sales budget, by quarter and by product, for the year ending 31 December. Calculations: prices per unit to the nearest cent; all other figures to the nearest whole number.

Endnotes

1 Heizer, J. and Render, B., *Production and Operations Management Strategies and Tactics*, 3rd edn, Needham Heights, USA: Allyn & Bacon, 1993, p. 122
2 Hilton, R., *Managerial Accounting*, 2nd edn, New York, USA: McGraw-Hill Book Company, 1994, p. 375
3 Adapted from Hilton

Chapter 3

Operating budgets for service organisations

Introduction

Operating budgets are those budgets that estimate activities which will affect profit. Typically, for a merchandising firm, these budgets are:

- sales budget
- purchases budget
- cost of goods sold budget
- marketing (or selling and distribution) expenses budget
- administration (and general) expenses budget
- financial expenses budget.

Sales budgets are normally the starting point in the preparation of the budgets listed above. Sales budgets were dealt with in Chapter 2. The remaining operating budgets will be covered in this chapter.

The operating budgets are prepared so that their details can be included in the budgeted revenue statement. Remember that a revenue statement is the combination of a trading statement and a profit and loss statement. Although the budgeted revenue statement is a financial statement and not an operating statement, it is introduced later in this chapter in order to show how operating budgets are integrated into budgeted revenue statements.

Tough as Teak is to commence business as a retail store, specialising in wooden furniture, on 1 April. The store is operated by its owners, Janice and Eron Roberts, supported by casual staff. Budgets which Tough as Teak need to prepare are shown in Figure 3.1. The preparation of Tough as Teak's operating budgets will be the subject of much of this chapter.

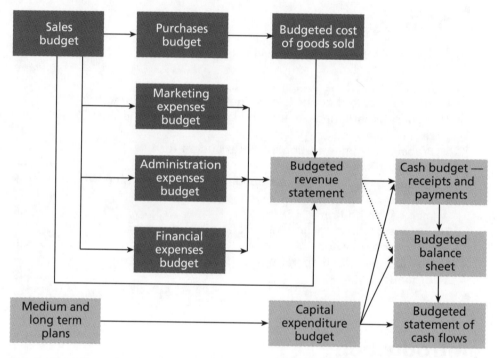

Figure 3.1 *Master budget for Tough as Teak — operating budgets highlighted*

Purchases budget

The purchases budget shows the purchases necessary to satisfy anticipated sales and desired inventory levels. Details from the purchases budget can be used to prepare the cost of goods sold budget, which, in turn, forms part of the budgeted revenue statement.

As with sales budgets, purchases budgets can be prepared by product, by period, by area or some combination of these. Purchases budgets can be prepared in dollars or units.

The sales budget for Tough as Teak for April to July shows:

	$
April	43 000
May	38 000
June	41 000
July	39 000

Tough as Teak has a mark-up of 100% on cost. Management has a policy that beginning inventory is to be 120% of cost of sales for each month.

The purchases budget for the three months ending 30 June is prepared according to the following steps.

Step 1

Find the cost value of sales.

As the mark-up on cost is 100%, cost must be 50% of the sales figure, therefore:

April	$43 000 × 50% = $21 500
May	$38 000 × 50% = $19 000
June	$41 000 × 50% = $20 500

Step 2

Calculate beginning inventory values.

These values are calculated on the cost of sales because inventory is valued at cost.

April	$21 500 × 120% = $25 800
May	$19 000 × 120% = $22 800
June	$20 500 × 120% = $24 600

Step 3

Establish ending inventory values.

As the closing inventory for one month is the opening inventory for the following month, the closing inventory for April and May are $22 800 and $24 600 respectively. For June it is necessary to use estimated sales for July. July cost of sales is ($39 000 × 50%) $19 500. So the closing inventory for June is ($19 500 × 120%) $23 400.

Step 4

Prepare the purchases budget.

Tough as Teak

Purchases budget for the 3 months ending 30 June

	April $	May $	June $	Quarter $
Cost of sales	21 500	19 000	20 500	61 000
add Ending inventory	22 800	24 600	23 400	23 400
Total requirements	44 300	43 600	43 900	84 400
less Beginning inventory	25 800	22 800	24 600	25 800
To be purchased	18 500	20 800	19 300	58 600

Note that it is necessary to add the cost of sales to the ending inventory to establish the total requirements for the business. Some of these requirements are already on hand in the form of beginning inventory, the remainder represent the amount still to be purchased.

Also note that the inventory figures in the column headed 'Quarter' are the beginning and ending inventory figures for the quarter, *not* the totals of the respective rows. The 'Quarter' column and the 'To be purchased' row must cross-balance.

Self-test problem 3.1

The Oarsome Rowing Equipment Co. has estimated sales for January to April as:

	$
January	150 000
February	180 000
March	120 000
April	165 000

The mark-up on cost is 50% and management requires that opening stock be 90% of sales (at cost) each month.

Required
Prepare a purchases budget for the three months ending 31 March.

You should now be able to do Question 3.1

Purchases budget in units

To enable businesses to plan their ordering requirements it may be desirable to calculate the number of units to be purchased.

Consider Patrician Industries. Future sales, in units, have been estimated at:

January	60 000
February	55 000
March	65 000
April	62 000

Management requires that beginning inventory represents 80% of that month's sales. Selling price is $15 per unit. Purchase price is $10 per unit.

Before preparing the purchases budget (in units) it is necessary to calculate the desired inventories.

Calculation of inventories

		Units
1 January	(80% × 60 000)	48 000
1 February	(80% × 55 000)	44 000
1 March	(80% × 65 000)	52 000
1 April	(80% × 62 000)	49 600

Patrician Industries' purchases budget for the three months ending 31 March can now be prepared.

Patrician Industries

Purchases budget for the quarter ending 31 March

	January	February	March	Quarter
Sales (units)	60 000	55 000	65 000	180 000
add Ending inventory (units)	44 000	52 000	49 600	49 600
Total requirements (units)	104 000	107 000	114 600	229 600
less Beginning inventory (units)	48 000	44 000	52 000	48 000
Purchases (in units)	56 000	63 000	62 600	181 600
Cost per unit	x $10	x $10	x $10	x $10
Cost of purchases	$560 000	$630 000	$626 000	$1 816 000

The dollar value of beginning inventory, cost of goods sold, ending inventory and total requirements can all be found by multiplying each unit figure by the purchases price per unit.

Self-test problem 3.2

Framm Company has estimated the following sales:

	Units
April	3 000
May	3 300
June	3 200

Management requires a beginning inventory of 50% of that month's sales. Inventory at 30 June is expected to be 1500 units. Selling price is $250 per unit. Purchase price is $150 per unit.

Required
Prepare the purchases budget for the three months ending 30 June.

You should now be able to do Question 3.2

Purchases budget for multiple products

Where an organisation wishes to budget its purchases product by product, it may be necessary to prepare individual purchases budgets for each product. This would be the case if, say, a quarterly budget, showing monthly figures, was required. The individual budgets can then be consolidated into a total budget.

Gourmet Biscuits will be used to illustrate a consolidated purchases budget. Gourmet Biscuits' sales budget for the next financial year is:

Gourmet Biscuits

Sales budget for the year ending 30 June			
Type of biscuit	Sales volume kg	Sales price $	Sales $
Sweet Hearts	45 000	8.30	373 500
Cherry Surprises	41 000	7.30	299 300
Chocolate Supremes	57 000	6.25	356 250
Almond Delights	32 250	5.20	167 700
			1 196 750

Gourmet Biscuits' mark-up on cost is 50%. Inventories are anticipated to be:

Type of biscuit	1 July $	30 June $
Sweet Hearts	3 000	3 300
Cherry Surprises	2 500	2 700
Chocolate Supremes	2 900	3 200
Almond Delights	1 400	1 500

Gourmet Biscuits' consolidated purchases budget appears below:

Gourmet Biscuits

Purchases budget for the year ending 30 June					
	Sweet Hearts $	Cherry Surprises $	Chocolate Supremes $	Almond Delights $	Total $
Cost of sales	249 000	199 533	237 500	111 800	797 833
add Ending inventory	3 300	2 700	3 200	1 500	10 700
Total requirements	252 300	202 233	240 700	113 300	808 533
less Beginning inventory	3 000	2 500	2 900	1 400	9 800
To be purchased	249 300	199 733	237 800	111 900	798 733

Self-test problem 3.3

Romanesque Fragrances Ltd has produced the following sales budget for the coming financial year.

Romanesque Fragrances Ltd

Sales budget for the year ending 30 June

Type of perfume	Sales volume Litres	Sales price $	Sales $
Venus	3 600	376	1 353 600
Romantic Holiday	5 100	329	1 677 900
Balmy Breezes	7 600	220	1 672 000
			4 703 500

Romanesque Fragrances has a mark-up on cost of 100%. Beginning inventory is estimated to be 8% of the year's cost of sales for each product. Ending inventory should be 10% higher than beginning inventory.

Required
Prepare the purchases budget for the coming financial year.

You should now be able to do Question 3.3

Cost of goods sold budget

The format for the cost of goods sold budget is similar to the cost of goods sold section of a trading statement or revenue statement. This budget is required for the budgeted revenue statement.

Using information from the Tough as Teak's purchases budget compiled earlier, the cost of goods sold budget is as shown below:

Tough as Teak

Cost of goods sold budget for the 3 months ending 30 June

	April $	May $	June $	Quarter $
Beginning inventory	25 800	22 800	24 600	25 800
Purchases	18 500	20 800	19 300	58 600
Goods available for sale	44 300	43 600	43 900	84 400
less Ending inventory	22 800	24 600	23 400	23 400
Cost of goods sold	21 500	19 000	20 500	61 000

Self-test problem 3.4

Refer to Self-test problem 3.1.

Required
Prepare a cost of goods sold budget for the three months ending 31 March.

You should now be able to do Questions 3.4 and 3.5

Budgets for operating expenses

Recall from earlier studies that operating expenses in the profit and loss statement were categorised as marketing (or selling and distribution), administrative and financial.

It is necessary to prepare budgets for each of these categories so that the forecasted amounts of these expenses can be included in the budgeted revenue statement.

- **Marketing expenses** are those expenses which relate to attracting sales, making sales and delivering products. Examples of expenses for this category are advertising, selling commission and cartage outward.
- **Administration expenses** are those expenses which relate to the general office and the overall administration of the organisation. Expenses typical of this category are salaries of executives, office staff wages, stationery, rent and/or rates of office premises and depreciation of office furniture and equipment.
- **Financial expenses** relate to financial aspects of the business. Typical expenses included here are wages and salaries for credit department staff, bad debts, interest on loans and discount allowed.

Expense details for Tough as Teak are listed below. This information will be used to illustrate the marketing expenses budget, the administration expenses budget and the financial expenses budget for the three months ending 30 June.

Expense details

Casual salesperson's wages	$24 000 pa apportioned equally each month
Sales commissions	5% of sales
Advertising	2% of sales
Stationery	$600 pa apportioned equally each month
Telephone	$1200 pa apportioned equally each month
Superannuation	6% of total payroll
Workers' compensation insurance	8% of total payroll
Rent	$21 600 pa apportioned equally each month
Accountancy fees	$1800 pa apportioned equally each month
Depreciation (straight line method)	
Motor vehicle (used for deliveries)	20% pa on cost of $45 000
Shop fittings	15% pa on cost of $30 000
Office furniture and equipment	15% pa on cost of $16 000
Interest on loan	
April	$600
May	$587
June	$573
Bank charges, debits tax and financial institutions duty	$480 pa apportioned equally each month

Marketing expenses budget

It is necessary to identify which expenses should be included in this budget. For Tough as Teak, casual salesperson's wages, sales commissions, advertising, depreciation on shop fittings and depreciation on delivery vehicle are all obvious. In this instance superannuation and workers' compensation insurance are included as the entire payroll relates to sales staff. This will not always be the case.

The following table indicates the amount applicable for each of these expenses and their calculations for the months of April, May and June.

Expense	April	May	June
Salesperson's wages	$24 000/12 = $2000	$2000	$2000
Sales commissions	5% × $43 000 = $2150	5% × $38 000 = $1900	5% × $41 000 = $2050
Advertising	2% × $43 000 = $860	2% × $38 000 = $760	2% × $41 000 = $820
Superannuation	($2000 + $2150) × 6% = $249	($2000 + $1900) × 6% = $234	($2000 + $2050) × 6% = $243
Workers' compensation insurance	($2000 + $2150) × 8% = $332	($2000 + $1900) × 8% = $312	($2000 + $2050) × 8% = $324
Depreciation on delivery vehicle	20% × $45 000/12 = $750	$750	$750
Depreciation on shop fittings	15% × $30 000/12 = $375	$375	$375

The marketing expenses budget for Tough as Teak is shown below:

Tough as Teak

Marketing expenses budget for the 3 months ending 30 June			
	April $	May $	June $	Quarter $
Salesperson's wages	2 000	2 000	2 000	6 000
Sales commissions	2 150	1 900	2 050	6 100
Advertising	860	760	820	2 440
Superannuation	249	234	243	726
Workers' compensation insurance	332	312	324	968
Depreciation:				
Delivery van	750	750	750	2 250
Shop fittings	375	375	375	1 125
Total marketing expenses	6 716	6 331	6 562	19 609

Self-test problem 3.5

Refer to Self-test problem 3.1. The Oarsome Rowing Equipment Co. provides you with the following information relating to estimated expenses.

Expense details

Sales representatives' salaries	$72 000 pa apportioned equally each month
Cartage outwards	5% of sales
Advertising	3% of sales
General salaries and wages	$144 000 pa apportioned equally each month
Audit fees	$2400 pa apportioned equally each month
Payroll on-costs (treated as an administration expense)	15% of total payroll
Rent	$43 200 pa apportioned equally each month
Depreciation	$27 600 pa apportioned equally each month
Telephone	$1800 pa apportioned equally each month
Stationery	$1800 pa apportioned equally each month
Interest on loan	January — $830 February — $820 March — $810
Bank charges etc	$720 pa apportioned equally each month

Required
Prepare the marketing expenses budget for the three months ending 31 March.

You should now be able to do Question 3.6

Administration expenses budget

The procedure adopted to prepare the marketing expenses budget will now be used to prepare the administration expenses budget.

Step 1

Identify administration expenses. In the Tough as Teak example these are stationery, telephone, rent, accountancy fees, and depreciation on office furniture and equipment.

Step 2

Calculate the monthly amount for each expense.

Stationery	$600/12 = $50 per month
Telephone	$1200/12 = $100 per month
Rent	$21 600/12 = $1800 per month
Accountancy fees	$1800/12 = $150 per month
Depreciation: office furniture and equipment	$15% × $16 000/12 = $200 per month

Step 3

Prepare the administration expenses budget.

Tough as Teak

Administration expenses budget for the 3 months ending 30 June

	April $	May $	June $	Quarter $
Stationery	50	50	50	150
Telephone	100	100	100	300
Rent	1 800	1 800	1 800	5 400
Accountancy fees	150	150	150	450
Depreciation:				
Office furniture				
and equipment	200	200	200	600
Total administration				
expenses	2 300	2 300	2 300	6 900

Self-test problem 3.6

Refer to Self-test problem 3.5.

Required

Prepare the administration expenses budget for the three months ending 31 March.

You should now be able to do Question 3.7

Financial expenses budget

The appropriate expenses need to be identified and their respective monthly amounts computed to enable the financial expenses budget to be prepared.

Tough as Teak

Financial expenses budget for the 3 months ending 30 June

	April $	May $	June $	Quarter $
Interest on loan	600	587	573	1 760
Bank charges etc	40	40	40	120
Total financial				
expenses	640	627	613	1 880

Self-test problem 3.7

Refer to Self-test problem 3.5.

Required
Prepare the financial expenses budget for the three months ending 31 March.

You should now be able to do Question 3.8

Budgeted revenue statement

To demonstrate the integration of operating budgets the budgeted revenue statement for Tough as Teak will now be prepared. Budgeted revenue statements can be prepared in summary form or in detail.

Summary budgeted revenue statement

In this format the totals from each of the operations budgets are combined into one statement as follows:

Tough as Teak

Budgeted revenue statement for the 3 months ending 30 June

	April $	May $	June $	Quarter $
Sales	43 000	38 000	41 000	122 000
less Cost of goods sold	21 500	19 000	20 500	61 000
Gross profit	21 500	19 000	20 500	61 000
less Operating expenses				
Marketing expenses	6 716	6 331	6 562	19 609
Administration expenses	2 300	2 300	2 300	6 900
Financial expenses	640	627	613	1 880
Total operating expenses	9 656	9 258	9 475	28 389
Net profit	11 844	9 742	11 025	32 611

Self-test problem 3.8

Refer to Self-test problems 3.1 and 3.4 to 3.7.

Required
Prepare a summary budgeted revenue statement for the three months ending 31 March.

Detailed budgeted revenue statement

The individual operating budgets, showing detailed information, are combined into one statement as shown below:

Tough as Teak

Budgeted revenue statement for the 3 months ending 30 June

	April $	May $	June $	Quarter $
Sales	43 000	38 000	41 000	122 000
less **Cost of goods sold**				
Beginning inventory	25 800	22 800	24 600	25 800
Purchases	18 500	20 800	19 300	58 600
Goods available for sale	44 300	43 600	43 900	84 400
less Ending inventory	22 800	24 600	23 400	23 400
Cost of goods sold	21 500	19 000	20 500	61 000
Gross profit	**21 500**	**19 000**	**20 500**	**61 000**
less **Operating expenses**				
Marketing expenses				
Salesperson's wages	2 000	2 000	2 000	6 000
Sales commissions	2 150	1 900	2 050	6 100
Advertising	860	760	820	2 440
Superannuation	249	234	243	726
Workers' compensation insurance	332	312	324	968
Depreciation:				
Delivery van	750	750	750	2 250
Shop fittings	375	375	375	1 125
	6 716	6 331	6 562	19 609
Administration expenses				
Stationery	50	50	50	150
Telephone	100	100	100	300
Rent	1 800	1 800	1 800	5 400
Accountancy fees	150	150	150	450
Depreciation:				
Office furniture and equipment	200	200	200	600
	2 300	2 300	2 300	6 900
Financial expenses				
Interest on loan	600	587	573	1 760
Bank charges etc	40	40	40	120
	640	627	613	1 880
Total operating expenses	9 656	9 258	9 475	28 389
Net profit	**11 844**	**9 742**	**11 025**	**32 611**

Self-test problem 3.9

Refer to Self-test problems 3.1 and 3.4 to 3.7.

Required
Prepare a detailed budgeted revenue statement for the three months ending 31 March.

You should now be able to do Questions 3.9 and 3.10

Professional services

Wimble, Tensby and Associates, accountants, were introduced in Chapter 2. Figure 3.2 shows the budgets used by this firm.

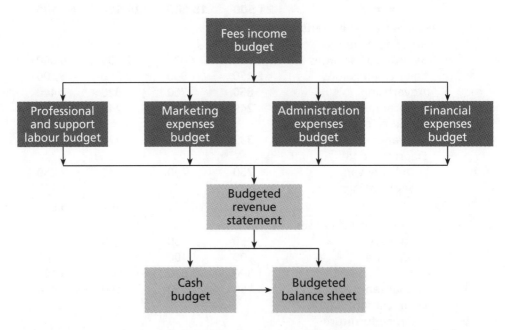

Figure 3.2 *Master budget for Wimble, Tensby and Associates — operating budgets highlighted*

As the preparation of the marketing expenses, administration expenses and financial expenses budgets is similar to those of merchandising firms only the professional and support labour budget will be illustrated.

Budgeted client hours are 950 for July, 980 for August and 995 for September. Professional labour costs an average of $45 per hour and support labour averages $25 per hour. It is estimated that 40% of client hours will require professional labour. Support labour will service the remaining 60%.

The professional and support labour budget will now be prepared.

Wimble, Tensby and Associates

**Professional and support labour budget
for the 3 months ending 30 September**

	July	August	September	Quarter
Professional labour hours	380	392	398	1 170
Average cost per hour	x $45	x $45	x $45	x $45
Professional labour	$17 100	$17 640	$17 910	$52 650
Support labour hours	570	588	597	1 755
Average cost per hour	x $25	x $25	x $25	x $25
Support labour	$14 250	$14 700	$14 925	$43 875
Total	$31 350	$32 340	$32 835	$96 525

Self-test problem 3.10

Manners and Fitzloon, solicitors, have asked you to prepare a professional and support labour budget. Estimated client hours for the coming quarter are: 1700 for month 1; 1800 for month 2; 1760 for month 3. Professional labour costs an average of $55 per hour and is expected to represent 45% of total hours charged to clients. Support labour costs should average $30 per hour with a 5% increase in the third month. Support labour is expected to represent 55% of total hours charged.

Required
Prepare a professional and support labour budget.

You should now be able to do Questions 3.11 and 3.12

Specialised service industry budgets

Service organisations may have specialised operating budgets. For example, hairdressers may have salon expenses and doctors may have surgery expenses.

Some service providers may also have stocks of goods. Recall the naturopath from Chapter 2. Carol Dewar carries and sells a line of herbs, vitamins and minerals. Carol would need a cost of goods sold budget. Similarly, builders, car repairers and others hold materials and charge these out to jobs. Appropriate budgets would be prepared for each of these examples.

Consider the case of Len Cannon, carpenter. Len believes that stock of materials on hand at the beginning of next year will be $10 500 and at the end of the year $17 000. Estimated purchase of materials are $53 000. The budgeted materials to be used next year are:

Len Cannon

Materials usage budget for the year ending ...

	$
Opening stock	10 500
Purchases	53 000
	63 500
less Closing stock	17 000
Materials usage	46 500

Self-test problem 3.11

Helen Bennett is a gardener and landscaper. She provides you with the following garden and landscape supplies information for the coming year:

* beginning inventory $5100
* purchases $21 300
* ending inventory $5500.

Required
Prepare a budget showing estimated usage of garden and landscape supplies for the coming year.

You should now be able to do Questions 3.13 to 3.16

Checklist

Before progressing to the next chapter, complete the checklist below. This will identify whether you have an understanding of the important parts of the chapter.

Can you do the following?

☐ Prepare a purchases budget for a merchandising firm
☐ Prepare a cost of goods sold budget for a merchandising firm
☐ Prepare a marketing expenses budget for a merchandising firm
☐ Prepare an administration expenses budget for a merchandising firm
☐ Prepare a financial expenses budget for a merchandising firm
☐ Prepare a simple budgeted revenue statement for a merchandising firm
☐ Prepare professional and support labour budgets for professional services
☐ Prepare specialised operating budgets for particular service organisations

Questions

3.1 Orlando Groceries estimated sales for October to February are:

	$
October	72 000
November	69 000
December	81 000
January	75 000
February	72 000

The mark-up on cost is 20%. Management requires that beginning inventory is to be 60% of that month's cost of sales plus 40% of the next month's cost of sales.

Required

Prepare a purchases budget for the three months ending 31 December.

3.2 Expected sales for Fisher Wholesalers are:

	Units
July	14 700
August	15 120
September	15 680
October	16 240

Each month's closing inventory is to be 150% of the following month's sales. Average selling price is $30 per unit. Average cost of purchases is $20 per unit.

Required

Prepare for the three months July, August and September:

(a) a sales budget, and
(b) a purchases budget.

3.3 Alzaria Products presents you with the following sales budget for the next financial year.

Alzaria Products

Sales budget for the year ending 30 June			
Product	**Sales volume** Litres	**Sales price** $	**Sales** $
Siluria	108 000	10.50	1 134 000
Malus	52 000	7.35	382 200
Zyton	75 200	8.40	631 680
			2 147 880

Alzaria Products has a mark-up on cost of 75%. Beginning inventories are estimated at: Siluria — $64 800; Malus — $17 500; Zyton — $39 700. Ending inventories are anticipated to vary from beginning inventories by: Siluria — a decrease of 15%; Malus — an increase of 10%; Zyton — a decrease of 10%.

Required

Prepare the purchases budget for the coming financial year.

3.4 Refer to Question 3.2. Prepare a cost of goods sold budget for the three months ending 30 September.

3.5 Y. Friend provides you with the following details.

Budgeted sales income

	$
October	600 000
November	800 000
December	900 000
January	700 000

Sale price per unit is 175% of cost price. The opening inventory value for each month should be 75% of the budgeted cost of sales for that month.

Required

For the three months ending 31 December prepare:

(a) a purchases budget, and

(b) a cost of goods sold budget.

3.6 Refer to Question 3.2. Fisher Wholesalers provides you with estimated expense details as follows:

Expense details

Administrative wages and salaries	$432 000 pa apportioned equally each month
Audit fees	$12 000 pa apportioned equally each month
Bad debts	1% of sales
Bank charges etc	$3840 pa apportioned equally each month
Credit department staff wages	$78 000 pa apportioned equally each month
Depreciation (straight line method)	
Motor vehicles	20% pa on $150 000
Office equipment	15% pa on $100 000
Warehouse fixtures and	
equipment	15% pa on $130 000
Labour on-costs	16% of payroll — to be allocated to each expense classification
Rent	$86 400 pa apportioned equally each month
Sales commissions	5% of sales
Salespersons' wages	$288 000 pa apportioned equally each month
Telephone and stationery	$18 000 pa apportioned equally each month

Required

Prepare a marketing expenses budget for the three months ending 30 September.

3.7 Refer to Question 3.6. Prepare an administration expenses budget for the three months ending 30 September.

3.8 Refer to Question 3.6. Prepare a financial expenses budget for the three months ending 30 September.

3.9 Refer to Questions 3.2, 3.4 and 3.6 to 3.8.

(a) Prepare a summary budgeted revenue statement for the three months ending 30 September.

(b) Prepare a detailed budgeted revenue statement for the three months ending 30 September.

3.10 Acamas Traders has asked you to prepare its operating budgets for the coming year. You are provided with the following information:

	1st quarter	2nd quarter	3rd quarter	4th quarter
Sales (in units)	65 000	80 000	90 000	100 000
Sales manager's salary	$15 000	$15 000	$15 000	$16 500
Administration salaries	$60 000	$60 000	$66 000	$66 000
Insurances	$3 000	$3 000	$3 000	$3 000
Rent	$3 500	$3 500	$3 500	$3 500
Depreciation of equipment	$2 000	$2 000	$2 000	$2 000
Miscellaneous expenses	$13 100	$13 200	$13 300	$13 400
Interest expense	$14 000	$13 000	$12 000	$11 000

- Advertising — $1.50 per unit
- Sales commissions — 5% of sales
- Bad debts — 2% of sales
- Average selling price per unit is $12
- Acamas has a mark-up of 100% on cost
- Beginning inventory should be 80% of that quarter's sales
- Estimated sales for the first quarter of the year following the budget year are 70 000 units

Required

Prepare the following by quarter for the coming year:

(a) sales budget
(c) purchases budget
(c) cost of goods sold budget
(d) marketing expenses budget
(e) administration expenses budget
(f) financial expenses budget
(g) summary budgeted revenue statement.

3.11 City Dental Associates is a large dental practice in Brisbane. The firm's accountant is preparing the budget for the next year. He projects a total of 48 000 patient visits, to be evenly distributed throughout the year. Eighty per cent of the visits will be half hour appointments, and the remainder will be one hour visits. City dentists earn $50 per hour, this rate is due to increase by 10% in May of next year. Prepare a professional labour budget, by month, for the quarter ending 30 June next year.[1]

3.12 Budgeted fees income for Bridge Street Medical Centre for the six months ending 31 December is:

	$
July	266 760
August	326 040
September	311 220
October	296 400
November	355 680
December	281 580

It is estimated that professional labour will be 35% of income and support labour will be 25%. Prepare a professional and support labour budget for the half year ending 31 December.

3.13 Katherine Hartley is a dentist. She provides you with next year's estimates for drugs and fillings etc which she keeps in stock.

	$
Opening stock	8 000
Closing stock	10 000
Purchases	5 000

Prepare a usages budget for drugs and fillings etc for the coming year.

3.14 Bob Bertram needs materials for his building business. He estimates his usage for the next four months will be: $41 800 in month 1; $34 200 in month 2; $39 900 in month 3; $35 600 in month 4. He wants opening stock to represent 75% of the month's usage. Prepare a building materials purchases budget for the three months ending month 3.

3.15 Below is information relating to Dr M. Way for the coming year.

	$
Accounting fees	1 000
Depreciation of office equipment	900
Depreciation of surgery equipment	2 500
Drugs, medications and dressings: expected usage	5 200
Replacement of surgical and medical instruments	1 600

(continued on next page)

	$
(continued from previous page)	
Laundry and cleaning	4 000
Light and power	2 000
Motor vehicle lease	15 600
Motor vehicle running expenses	8 400
Professional association fees	1 000
Rent	38 400
Stationery and postage	800
Wages:	
Clerk/receptionist	21 200
Surgery nurse	32 600

Light and power and rent are allocated 75% to the surgery and 25% to the office.

Required

Prepare the following for the coming year:

(a) surgery expenses budget
(b) administration expenses budget
(c) general expenses budget.

3.16 Melanie Street operates a hairdressing salon. Some figures for last year are shown below:

	$
Advertising	2 000
Bank charges etc	300
Cleaning	2 600
Depreciation:	
Office equipment	1 000
Salon equipment	2 500
Hairdressers' wages	60 000
Hairdressing implements — replacement	400
Hairdressing materials used	9 000
Interest on loan	5 000
Light and power	3 000
Office staff wages	20 000
Rent	26 000
Stationery and postage	500

- The budget for next year anticipates the following changes: advertising — increase of 2%; bank charges etc — increase of 3%; cleaning — decrease of 10%; hairdresser's wages — increase of 5%; hairdressing implements replacement — decrease of 10%; hairdressing materials used — increase of 7%; interest on loan — decrease of 20%; light and power — increase of 4%; office staff wages — increase of 5%; rent — increase of 10%; stationery and postage — decrease of 5%.

- Cleaning, light and power and rent are allocated 80% to the salon and 20% to the office.
- Depreciation of office equipment and depreciation of salon equipment remain unchanged.

Required

Prepare an operating expenses budget with appropriate cost classifications, for the coming year.

Endnote

1 Adapted from Langfield-Smith, K., Thorne, H. and Hilton, R., *Management Accounting: An Australian Perspective*, Sydney, NSW: McGraw-Hill Book Company, 1995

Chapter 4

Cash budgets for service organisations

Objectives

By the end of this chapter you will be able to:

Introduction

In Chapter 1 the distinction was made between cash budgets and budgeted statements of cash flows. Recall that a *budgeted statement of cash flows* is the estimated cash flows for a future period presented in the specific format required by accounting standards AAS 28 and AASB 1026, both entitled, *Statement of Cash Flows*. A **cash budget** shows the predicted cash receipts and payments, and cash balance or balances for a given period or periods.

This chapter deals only with cash budgets. Initially businesses operating on a purely cash basis are considered. Later businesses that receive and grant credit are explored.

Budgeted statements of cash flows are introduced in Chapter 5.

Cash receipts budget

Carol Dewar, naturopath, has prepared the following revenue budget for the quarter ending 30 September.

Carol Dewar

Revenue budget for the quarter ending 30 September

	July $	August $	September $	Total for the quarter $
Consultation fees				
Normal	10 290	9 870	8 960	29 120
Home visits	2 220	2 100	1 920	6 240
Fees income	12 510	11 970	10 880	35 360
Sales				
Vitamins and minerals	1 750	1 430	1 310	4 490
Herbal remedies	1 450	1 550	1 430	4 430
Sales income	3 200	2 980	2 740	8 920
Other income				
Rental income	500	500	500	1 500
Investment interest			150	150
Total other income	500	500	650	1 650
Total revenue	16 210	15 450	14 270	45 930

Carol's cash receipts budget appears below. Remember, Carol operates on a strictly cash basis:

Carol Dewar

Cash receipts budget for the quarter ending 30 September

	July $	August $	September $	Total for the quarter $
Consultation fees received	12 510	11 970	10 880	35 360
Cash sales	3 200	2 980	2 740	8 920
Rental income	500	500	500	1 500
Investment interest			150	150
Total cash receipts	16 210	15 450	14 270	45 930

Self-test problem 4.1

St Jude's Musical Academy has the following revenue budget for the quarter ending 31 March.

St Jude's Musical Academy

Revenue budget for the quarter ending 31 March

	January $	February $	March $	Total $
Fees income				
Guitar lessons	5 800	5 400	6 200	17 400
Piano lessons	6 600	5 900	5 900	18 400
Woodwind and brass lessons	2 400	2 000	2 600	7 000
Total fees income	14 800	13 300	14 700	42 800
Sales of instruments				
Guitars	1 000	800	1 200	3 000
Woodwind and brass	600	800	900	2 300
Total sales	1 600	1 600	2 100	5 300
Total revenue	16 400	14 900	16 800	48 100

St Jude's operates on a strictly cash basis.

Required
Prepare a cash receipts budget for the quarter ending 31 March.

You should now be able to do Question 4.1

Cash payments budget

While preparing her budgets, Carol Dewar estimated expense details as follows.

Purchases of oils, minerals, vitamins and herbs	$24 000 incurred evenly throughout the year
Rent	$1500 per month
Laundry	$1800 incurred evenly throughout the year
Telephone	$200 per quarter payable in March, June, September and December
Insurances	$1200 payable in August
Stationery	January — $150 July — $200

Motor vehicle running costs	$0.70 per km
	Estimated for the coming quarter
	    July — 230 km
	    August — 210 km
	    September — 190 km

Depreciation	$2400 pa

Carol intends to purchase a new massage table in July at a cost of $300.

Carol's cash payments budget for the quarter ending September is shown below. Remember, Carol is operating on a strictly cash basis.

Carol Dewar

Cash payments budget for the quarter ending 30 September

	July	August	September	Total for the quarter
	$	$	$	$
Purchases	2 000	2 000	2 000	6 000
Rent	1 500	1 500	1 500	4 500
Laundry	150	150	150	450
Telephone			200	200
Insurances		1 200		1 200
Stationery	200			200
Motor vehicle running cost	161	147	133	441
Massage table	300			300
Total cash payments	4 311	4 997	3 983	13 291

Note that depreciation has been excluded as it is simply a book entry and does not involve the payment of cash. Also observe that items are included in the month that the payment is expected to take place.

Self-test problem 4.2

Melanie Street operates a hairdressing salon. She has asked you to prepare a cash payments budget for the quarter ending 30 June. You are provided with the following information.

Advertising	April — $170 May — $160 June — $200
Bank charges etc	$300 incurred evenly throughout the year
Cleaning	April — $190 May — $200 June — $190
Depreciation	Office equipment — $1200 pa Salon equipment — $2400 pa
Hairdressers' wages	April — $5200 May — $5250 June — $5300
Replacement of hairdressing implements	May — $180
Purchase of hairdressing materials	April — $800 May — $850 June — $820

(continued on next page)

(continued from previous page)

Interest on loan	April — $510 May — $440 June — $360
Light and power	$780 payable in April
Office staff wages	$1750 per month
Rent	April — $2160 May — $2160 June — $2400
Stationery and postage	$120 paid in June
Insurances	$1500 paid in May

- Melanie intends purchasing new salon equipment in April at a cost of $1500.
- Melanie's business operates on a strictly cash basis.

Required
Prepare the cash payments budget for the quarter ending 30 June.

You should now be able to do Question 4.2

Format for the cash budget

The basic format for a cash budget is:

- opening balance
- *add* receipts
- cash available
- *less* payments
- closing balance.

Using Carol Dewar's cash receipts and cash payments budgets illustrated earlier, it is now possible to prepare a cash budget. The opening balance on 1 July is expected to be $2390 cash at bank.

Carol Dewar

Cash budget for the quarter ending 30 September

	July $	August $	September $
Opening balance	2 390	14 289	24 742
add Receipts	16 210	15 450	14 270
Cash available for needs	18 600	29 739	39 012
less Payments	4 311	4 997	3 983
Closing balance	14 289	24 742	35 029

If the closing balance reveals a deficiency, this indicates that an overdraft or other finance will have to be arranged. Alternatively, cash payments could be deferred until funds are available.

Note that the closing balance for July becomes the opening balance for August, and so on.

The cash budget presented here was in summary format. If a detailed cash budget is prepared individual cash receipts and payments budgets are not necessary as the detail is included in the cash budget. Detailed cash budgets will be illustrated later in the chapter.

Self-test problem 4.3

Refer to Self-test problem 4.2.

- Estimated opening balance at 1 April is $1210.
- The cash receipts budget for the quarter ending 30 June showed total receipts as: April $9840; May $13 260; June $14 780.

Required
Prepare, in summary form, the cash budget for the quarter ending June.

You should now be able to do Question 4.3

Collections from accounts receivable

Very few organisations operate on a strictly cash basis. Most businesses receive credit and many grant credit. When this happens money owed may be paid at different times. Although a company may allow thirty days credit, some customers may take longer to pay or not pay at all.

When preparing cash budgets it is important to estimate when cash will actually be received or paid.

Consider the case of Dermott Jewellers. The company is preparing its cash budget for the quarter ending 31 March:

- 40% of Dermott's sales are for cash and the remainder are on credit
- records reveal that accounts receivable pay: 65% in the month following the sale; 30% in the second month after the sale; 5% in the third month after the sale.

Sales	$
Actual	
October	56 000
November	64 000
December	70 000
Budgeted	
January	66 000
February	52 000
March	68 000

To establish the likely cash receipts from accounts receivable, Josh Brown, budget accountant, adopted the following procedure:

Step 1

He calculated cash and credit sales.

	October $	November $	December $	January $	February $	March $
Cash sales (40%)	22 400	25 600	28 000	26 400	20 800	27 200
Credit sales (60%)	33 600	38 400	42 000	39 600	31 200	40 800
	56 000	64 000	70 000	66 000	52 000	68 000

Cash sales will be received in the month that the sales were made.

Step 2

Josh prepared a 'collection from accounts receivable' schedule.

Dermott Jewellers

Schedule of collections from accounts receivable for the quarter ending 31 March

		Month received		
Month of sale	$	January $	February $	March $
October	33 600			
November	38 400			
December	42 000			
January	39 600			
February	31 200			
March	40 800			
Total collections				

Note that calculations are based on credit sales.

Step 3

Josh calculated the remaining collections from October sales — 65% of October sales should have been collected in November and 30% in December. This leaves 5%, which should be collected in January (5% × $33 600 = $1680).

Dermott Jewellers

Schedule of collections from accounts receivable for the quarter ending 31 March

		Month received		
		January	February	March
Month of sale	$	$	$	$
October	33 600	(5%) 1 680		
November	38 400			
December	42 000			
January	39 600			
February	31 200			
March	40 800			
Total collections				

Step 4

Next, he calculated the remaining collections from November sales — 65% of November sales should have been collected in December. This means that 30% is estimated to be collected in January (30% × $38 400 = $11 520) and 5% in February (5% × $38 400 = $1920).

Dermott Jewellers

Schedule of collections from accounts receivable for the quarter ending 31 March

		Month received		
		January	February	March
Month of sale	$	$	$	$
October	33 600	(5%) 1 680		
November	38 400	(30%) 11 520	(5%) 1 920	
December	42 000			
January	39 600			
February	31 200			
March	40 800			
Total collections				

Step 5

He calculated collections from December sales:

- January 65% × $42 000 = $27 300
- February 30% × $42 000 = $12 600
- March 5% × $42 000 = $2100

Dermott Jewellers

Schedule of collections from accounts receivable for the quarter ending 31 March

		Month received		
		January	February	March
Month of sale	$	$	$	$
October	33 600	(5%) 1 680		
November	38 400	(30%) 11 520	(5%) 1 920	
December	42 000	**(65%) 27 300**	**(30%) 12 600**	**(5%) 2 100**
January	39 600			
February	31 200			
March	40 800			
Total collections				

Step 6

Josh then calculated collections from January sales:

- February 65% × $39 600 = $25 740
- March 30% × $39 600 = $11 880

The uncollected amount at the end of the quarter (5% × $39 600 = $1980) would be part of the balance of accounts receivable account as at 31 March.

Dermott Jewellers

Schedule of collections from accounts receivable for the quarter ending 31 March

		Month received		
		January	February	March
Month of sale	$	$	$	$
October	33 600	(5%) 1 680		
November	38 400	(30%) 11 520	(5%) 1 920	
December	42 000	(65%) 27 300	(30%) 12 600	(5%) 2 100
January	39 600		**(65%) 25 740**	**(30%) 11 880**
February	31 200			
March	40 800			
Total collections				

Step 7

He calculated collections from February sales:

- March 65% × $31 200 = $20 280

The uncollected amount at the end of the quarter (35% × $31 200 = $10 920) would be part of accounts receivable as at 31 March.

Dermott Jewellers

Schedule of collections from accounts receivable for the quarter ending 31 March

| | | Month received | | |
| | | January | February | March |
Month of sale	$	$	$	$
October	33 600	(5%) 1 680		
November	38 400	(30%) 11 520	(5%) 1 920	
December	42 000	(65%) 27 300	(30%) 12 600	(5%) 2 100
January	39 600		(65%) 25 740	(30%) 11 880
February	31 200			**(65%) 20 280**
March	40 800			
Total collections				

Step 8

Josh finalised the 'schedule of collections from accounts receivable'.

As the first collections from March credit sales will not occur until April nothing is received from these sales in the quarter under review.

To find the amount of cash collected from accounts receivable for each month simply total each month's column.

Dermott Jewellers

Schedule of collections from accounts receivable for the quarter ending 31 March

| | | Month received | | |
| | | January | February | March |
Month of sale	$	$	$	$
October	33 600	(5%) 1 680		
November	38 400	(30%) 11 520	(5%) 1 920	
December	42 000	(65%) 27 300	(30%) 12 600	(5%) 2 100
January	39 600		(65%) 25 740	(30%) 11 880
February	31 200			(65%) 20 280
March	40 800			
Total collections		40 500	40 260	34 260

Step 9

It is possible to establish the balance of the accounts receivable account by computing the amount still uncollected at the end of the quarter. Using the calculations made above, Josh estimated the balance at 31 March to be:

	$
From January sales	1 980
From February sales	10 920
From March sales	40 800
Balance as at 31 March	53 700

Step 10

The cash sales and collections from accounts receivable can now be transferred to the cash receipts budget or the cash receipts section of the cash budget. Assuming no other receipts, the cash receipts budget for Dermott Jewellers would be:

Dermott Jewellers

Cash receipts budget for the quarter ending 31 March

	January $	February $	March $	Total $
Cash sales	26 400	20 800	27 200	74 400
Collections from accounts receivable	40 500	40 260	34 260	115 020
Total cash receipts	66 900	61 060	61 460	189 420

Self-test problem 4.4

Fellini Fashions asks you to prepare its budgets for the quarter ending 30 September. They provide you with the following information:

Sales	$
Actual	
April	52 000
May	78 000
June	84 500
Estimated	
July	65 000
August	84 500
September	91 000

- 70% of total sales are for cash, the remainder are on credit
- the accounts receivable repayment pattern is: 50% in the month after sale; 40% in the second month after sale; 10% in the third month after sale.

Required
(a) Prepare a cash receipts budget for the quarter ending 30 September.
(b) Compute the balance of the accounts receivable account as at 30 September.

You should now be able to do Questions 4.4 to 4.6

Discount allowed and bad debts

The estimation of collections from accounts receivable can be complicated by firms offering discount for prompt payment and the fact that some debtors do not pay.

Suppose that Horus Hardware offers a discount to credit customers. Relevant details appear below:

Sales	$
Actual	
May	57 000
June	63 000
Estimated	
July	72 000
August	51 000
September	36 000

- sales are 70% on credit and 30% for cash
- accounts receivable are expected to pay to the following pattern: 25% in the month of sale — prompt payment discount is 10%; 20% in the month after sale — prompt payment discount is 5%; 30% in the month after sale — too late for discount; 20% in the second month after sale
- 5% bad debts are estimated.

The approach to the preparation of the schedule of collections from accounts receivable is similar to that already shown, but discount must be considered and bad debts omitted. If 5% discount is being offered, only 95% of the amount owed will be received if payment is made within the discount period.

Horus Hardware's schedule of collections from accounts receivable for the three months ending 30 September will now be prepared.

Step 1

Calculate cash and credit sales.

	May $	June $	July $	August $	September $
Cash sales (30%)	17 100	18 900	21 600	15 300	10 800
Credit sales (70%)	39 900	44 100	50 400	35 700	25 200
	57 000	63 000	72 000	51 000	36 000

Step 2

Calculate collections from credit sales.

		$
May sales	Received in July	20% × $39 900 = 7 980
June sales	Received in July	20% × $44 100 × 95% = 8 379
		30% × $44 100 = 13 230
		21 609
	Received in August	20% × $44 100 = 8 820
July sales	Received in July	25% × $50 400 × 90% = 11 340
	Received in August	20% × $50 400 × 95% = 9 576
		30% × $50 400 = 15 120
		24 696
	Received in September	20% × $50 400 = 10 080
August sales	Received in August	25% × $35 700 × 90% = 8 033
	Received in September	20% × $35 700 × 95% = 6 783
		30% × $35 700 = 10 710
		17 493
September sales	Received in September	25% × $25 200 × 90% = 5 670

As bad debts will not be collected they have been completely omitted.

Step 3

Prepare schedule of collections from accounts receivable.

Horus Hardware

**Schedule of collections from accounts receivable
for the quarter ending 30 September**

		Month received		
Month of sale	**$**	**July $**	**August $**	**September $**
May	39 900	7 980		
June	44 100	21 609	8 820	
July	50 400	11 340	24 696	10 080
August	35 700		8 033	17 493
September	25 200			5 670
Total collections		**40 929**	**41 549**	**33 243**

Self-test problem 4.5

Nuada Enterprises provides you with the following information:

Sales	$
Actual	
August	72 000
September	66 000
Budget	
October	90 000
November	108 000
December	96 000

- sales are 45% cash and 55% credit
- on average debtors pay to the following pattern: 40% in the month of sale — discount is 5%; 30% in the month following sale; 25% two months after sale
- 5% are estimated as bad debts.

Required
Prepare a schedule of collections from debtors for the quarter ending 31 December.

You should now be able to do Questions 4.7 and 4.8

Accounts payable and expenses

Accounts payable and expenses may not necessarily be paid in the month they are incurred. Schedules for payments to creditors and for expenses, similar to the schedule for collections from accounts receivable, should be prepared.

Self-test problem 4.6

Potamid's Pool Playthings provides the following information:

	$
Purchases for January (actual)	47 500
February (actual)	50 500
Ending inventory as at 28 February	63 000
Budgeted sales	
March	77 500
April	68 700
May	81 200
June	75 000

- cost of sales is 55% of sales — management wants beginning inventory to represent 100% of the cost of sales for that month plus 20% of the cost of sales for the next month
- purchases are paid for as follows: 40% in the month of purchase with a 5% discount; 50% in the following month; 10% two months after purchase.

Required

Prepare a schedule of payments for purchases for March and April. *Hint:* You will need to prepare a purchases budget.

You should now be able to do Questions 4.9 and 4.10

The cash budget

After preparing a sales budget, purchases budget, cost of goods sold budget, various expense budgets and schedules of collections from accounts receivable and payments to accounts payable, Apis Antiques prepared the following cash budget for the quarter ending 31 March.

Apis Antiques

Cash budget for the 3 months ending 31 March

	January $	February $	March $
Beginning cash balance — surplus/(deficiency)	(4 165)	14 994	(760)
Receipts			
Cash sales	37 240	23 422	28 567
Collections from accounts receivable	15 386	19 894	24 304
Total receipts	52 626	43 316	52 871
Cash available for needs	48 461	58 310	52 111
Payments			
Cash purchases	9 702	15 435	14 994
Accounts payable	12 495	25 015	10 657
Marketing expenses	5 600	5 600	5 600
Administration expenses	5 670	5 670	5 670
Equipment purchase		7 350	
Total payments	33 467	59 070	36 921
Closing cash balance — surplus/(deficiency)	**14 994**	**(760)**	**15 190**

It is acceptable for individual receipts and payments to be shown if management requires this level of detail.

Self-test problem 4.7

The following information is provided by Parvati Products:

Cash at bank — 30 September	$2550
Accounts payable — 30 September	$7650
Actual credit sales	July — $18 900 August — $14 700 September — $8100
Estimated credit sales	October — $13 200 November — $15 300 December — $11 400
Estimated cash sales	October — $22 800 November — $14 340 December — $17 490
Estimated credit purchases	October —$15 315 November — $6525 December — $12 855
Estimated cash purchases	October — $5940 November — $9450 December — $9180

- Debtors normally pay 80% in the month after sale; 20% two months after sale.
- Goods purchased on credit are paid for in the following month.
- Wages of $6900 are paid each month.
- Insurances of $4500 are due in December.

Required
Prepare a cash budget covering October, November and December.

You should now be able to do Questions 4.11 to 4.15

Desired balance and financial requirements

It is not unknown for management to require that a minimum desired cash at bank balance be achieved. This may mean borrowing funds to ensure that the desired balance is attained.

Suppose that Apis Antiques now requires a minimum cash balance of $10 000. Its cash budget would be restructured as follows.

Apis Antiques

Cash budget for the 3 months ending 31 March

	January $	February $	March $
(a) *Beginning cash balance — surplus/(deficiency)*	(4 165)	14 994	10 000
Receipts			
Cash sales	37 240	23 422	28 567
Collections from accounts receivable	15 386	19 894	24 304
(b) *Total receipts*	52 626	43 316	52 871
(c) *Cash available for needs* (a + b)	48 461	58 310	62 871
Payments			
Cash purchases	9 702	15 435	14 994
Accounts payable	12 495	25 015	10 657
Marketing expenses	5 600	5 600	5 600
Administration expenses	5 670	5 670	5 670
Equipment purchase		7 350	
(d) *Total payments*	33 467	59 070	36 921
(e) *Minimum desired balance*	10 000	10 000	10 000
(f) *Total cash needed* (d + e)	43 467	69 070	46 921
Cash surplus/(deficiency) (c – f)	4 994	10 760	15 950
Financing			
Borrowings	—	10 760*	—
Repayments	—	—	(10 760)
Interest	—	—	(90)†
(g) *Total effects of financing*	—	10 760	(10 850)
Closing cash balance — surplus/(deficiency) (c – d + g)	**14 994**	**10 000**	**15 100**

* Interest at 10% is payable only when repayments are made. The loan can be reduced by payments at any time, but must be repaid within six months

† $10 760 × 10%/12 = $90

Borrowings are made in the month that a deficit is likely to occur.

In this instance it was possible to repay the borrowings in the following month. This will not always be the case. Also, there may be conditions attached regarding the denominations of amounts that can be borrowed or repaid, for example, whole thousands of dollars. There may also be other stipulations regarding repayments and these must be taken into account when preparing the cash budget.

Excess funds may be invested, provided that the cash budget does not reveal that these funds will be required soon after the surplus occurs.

Self-test problem 4.8

Severe illness has struck down the budget accountant of Mayhew and Associates, a large legal firm. The partially completed cash budget for January and February appears below.

Mayhew and Associates

Cash budget for the 2 months ending 28 February

	January $	February $
Beginning cash balance	32 500	**(a)**
Collection of legal fees	162 500	187 000
Proceeds from sale of assets	**(b)**	2 250
Cash available for needs	230 750	**(c)**
Cash payments		
Salaries and wages	100 000	97 750
Other expenses	84 750	**(d)**
Purchases of assets	**(e)**	—
Total payments	210 750	179 000
Minimum desired balance	25 000	**(f)**
Total cash needed	**(g)**	204 000
Cash surplus/(deficiency)	(5 000)	**(h)**
Financing		
Borrowings	**(i)**	—
Repayment	—	**(j)**
Interest	—	**(k)**
Total effects of financing	**(l)**	(5 050)
Closing cash balance	**(m)**	30 200

To eliminate any cash deficiency Mayhew and Associates plan to borrow the exact amount required. The current interest rate is 12% per annum. Borrowings are repaid as soon as possible.

Required
Complete the cash budget by finding the missing figures identified by the letters **(a)** to **(m)** inclusive.

You should now be able to do Questions 4.16 to 4.19

Checklist

Before progressing to the next chapter, complete the checklist below. This will identify whether you have an understanding of the important parts of the chapter.

Can you do the following?

- ☐ Prepare cash receipts budgets for merchandising and other service organisations
- ☐ Prepare cash payments budgets for merchandising and other service organisations
- ☐ Prepare summary cash budgets for merchandising and other service organisations
- ☐ Estimate collections from accounts receivable
- ☐ Estimate payments to accounts payable and for expenses
- ☐ Prepare detailed cash budgets for merchandising and other service organisations
- ☐ Allow for a minimum desired cash balance and financing requirements, for merchandising and other service organisations

Questions

4.1 Day's Dental Surgery provides you with the following revenue budget.

Day's Dental Surgery

Revenue budget for the year ending 30 June

	1st quarter	2nd quarter	3rd quarter	4th quarter	Total
Professional services					
Surgery visits	900	1 000	940	980	
Average fee	$80	$80	$85	$85	
Fees income	$72 000	$80 000	$79 900	$83 300	$315 200
Sales — orthodontic devices					
Sales volume	50	70	60	55	
Average selling price	$100	$110	$110	$115	
Sales	$5 000	$7 700	$6 600	$6 325	$25 625
Other income					
Investment income	$3 000		$3 500		$6 500
Rental income	$1 000	$1 000	$1 100	$1 100	$4 200
Total other income	$4 000	$1 000	$4 600	$1 100	$10 700
Total revenue	$81 000	$88 700	$91 100	$90 725	$351 525

The surgery operates on a strictly cash basis.

Required

Prepare the cash receipts budget for the year ending 30 June.

4.2 Below is information relating to Dr M. Way for the quarter ending 31 December.

Accounting fees	$1000 pa paid each December

Depreciation:
  Office equipment
  Surgery equipment
	
	$900 pa
	$2500 pa

Purchase of drugs, medication and dressings	October — $430 November — $400 December — $450
Replacement of surgical and medical instruments	$800 payable in October
Laundry and cleaning	$330 per month
Light and power	$500 per quarter payable in November
Motor vehicle lease	$1300 per month
Motor vehicle running expenses	October — $710 November — $690 December — $740
Professional association fees	$1000 payable in December
Rent	$3200 per month
Stationery and postage	October — $150 November — $120

Wages:
  Clerk/receptionist
  Surgery nurse
	
	$1750 per month
	$2700 per month

Dr Way operates his practice on a strictly cash basis.

Required

Prepare a cash payments budget for the three months ending 31 December.

4.3 Refer to Question 4.2. The estimated opening bank balance at 1 October is $5350 overdrawn. Estimated cash receipts are: October $12 650; November $13 780; December $16 420. Prepare, in summary format, the cash budget for the quarter ending 31 December.

4.4 Actual and expected sales for Khepri Products are:

	Units
July	1340
August	1260
September	1200
October	1320
November	1300
December	1390

- Average selling price is $20 per unit.
- All sales are on credit.
- Collections from debtors follow a pattern: 10% in the month of sale; 70% in the month following sale; 20% two months after sale.

Required
(a) Prepare a schedule of collections from debtors for the three months ending 31 December.
(b) Compute the balance of the debtors account as at 31 December.

4.5 Dr N. Harding is a medical practitioner. Half of her patients pay by cash at the time of their visit; 30% pay by credit card; the remainder claim from their health fund first and then pay with the health fund cheque and make up any difference. Dr Harding receives payment from health fund claimants in the month following their visit. She receives payment from the credit card companies in the second month after the patient's visit. Estimated fees for the six months ending 30 June are:

	$
January	20 000
February	18 000
March	19 500
April	20 500
May	22 000
June	25 000

Required
(a) Prepare a schedule showing collection of fees for the three months ending 30 June.
(b) How much of the fees will remain uncollected at 30 June?

4.6 Behdety Sports Supplies is preparing its budgets for the quarter ending 31 March.

	$
Debtors balances at 1 January	
From October sales	2 000
From November sales	9 000
From December sales	23 000
Estimated sales	
January	39 000
February	43 500
March	42 000

- Cash sales are 50% of total sales.
- Credit sales are normally collected 60% in the month following sale, 30% in the second month after sale, and 10% in the third month after sale.
- Behdety also receives other income: $1500 rental income in January, February and March; $2100 investment interest in February.

Required

Prepare a cash receipts budget for the three months ending 31 March. Hint: Prepare a collection schedule first.

4.7 On 30 June Rahjid Patel had accounts receivable of $48 000 ($40 000 related to June sales).

Expected sales	Units
July	5250
August	5400
September	5600

- Selling price will be $8 per unit.
- Sales are invoiced on the last day of the month.
- Customers are allowed 4% discount if payment is made within 14 days.
- The pattern of receipts has been: 50% pay within the discount period; 30% pay within one month of being invoiced; 18% pay within two months of being invoiced; the remainder never pay.
- Other income — monthly interest of $1000 is received by Patel in respect of investments.

Required

(a) Prepare a cash receipts budget for the three months ending 30 September.
(b) Calculate the balance of accounts receivable as at 30 September. Assume no bad debts have been written off.

4.8 Sales for Lar Lingerie are:

	$
Actual	
February	8 000
March	10 000
Budget	
April	9 000
May	11 000
June	12 000

- Sales are 35% credit and 65% cash.
- Past experience indicates that collections are likely to be: 35% in the month of sale, with a 7.5% discount; 45% in the month following the sale; 15% in the second month after sale; 5% are uncollectable.

- Rental income is $1800 per month.
- In May it is estimated that $3000 will be received for commission on consignment sales.

Required

Prepare a cash receipts budget for the three months ending 30 June.

4.9 Refer to Question 4.7. Mr Patel provides additional information:
- The inventory balance at 30 June is $36 750.
- Accounts payable at 30 June figure is $17 100 — this is made up of May purchases $2000; June purchases $12 000; June expenses $3100.
- October sales are expected to be 5800 units with no change in sales price.
- Purchases: Each month's closing inventory is to be 140% of the following month's sales. Cost of purchases is $5 per unit. Purchases are paid 50% cash; 40% in the month after purchase; 10% two months after purchase.
- Other expenditure: Expenses are paid 75% in the month they occur and 25% in the following month. Marketing expenses are 18% of sales for each month (depreciation for marketing is $350). Administration expenses are 12% of sales for each month (depreciation for administration is $250 per month).

Required

Prepare a cash payments budget for the three months ending 30 September.

4.10 Shou-Hsing, purveyors of fine oriental cuisine, provide the following data:
- Purchases are paid 70% in the month following the purchase and 30% in the second month after the purchase.
- Other expenses are paid 65% in the month they are incurred and 35% in the next month.
- It is planned to purchase new furniture in April for $20 000.
- Payment of $160 000 income tax is due in May.
- Depreciation is $1000 per month.
- Actual and budgeted purchases and expenses are:

Month	Purchases $	Expenses $
November	50 000	43 500
December	62 500	45 000
January	50 000	43 750
February	45 000	45 500
March	45 000	37 500
April	47 500	35 000
May	52 500	30 000
June	51 000	36 000

Required

Prepare the cash payments budget for the six months ending 30 June.

4.11 Prepare a monthly cash budget for Encil Wholesalers for July, August and September using the information provided below.

- Expected receipts are:

	Cash sales $	Debtors $	Rent $	Plant $
July	37 000	38 750	5 000	
August	57 750	51 000	5 000	
September	52 500	63 250	5 000	15 000

- Purchases and expenses that appear in the budgeted revenue statement are:

	Purchases $	Expenses $
June	35 000	30 000
July	40 000	32 500
August	45 000	40 000
September	57 500	45 000

- Fifty per cent of expenses are paid in the month they are incurred. The balance of expenses and purchases are paid in the month following.
- Depreciation is $75 000 per annum.
- The bank account at 30 June is $12 500 overdraft.

4.12 Anu Enterprises expects to commence the calendar year with the following assets:

	$
Cash at bank	33 750
Inventory (at cost)	70 500
Land	75 000
Plant (at cost)	720 000
Debtors	75 000

- Note that the debtors balance will represent 25% of the credit sales for the previous December.
- Sales are estimated as:

	$
January	270 000
February	450 000
March	810 000
April	825 000

- The sales collection is expected to follow that of previous months: 40% of sales have been on a cash basis with these customers receiving an immediate cash discount of 2%; the remainder of sales are on credit and these customers do not receive any discounts.
- The previous collection pattern is expected to continue: 75% collected in the month of sale; 24% in the next month after sale; 1% uncollectable.
- Purchases are all for cash and receive a discount of 5%. Budgeted purchases are:

	$
January	180 000
February	345 000
March	517 500
April	628 500

- Monthly selling expenses are budgeted at: $36 000 fixed; variable — 10% of sales.
- Monthly administrative expenses are estimated as: $25 500 (including depreciation on plant) fixed; variable — 3% of sales.
- Depreciation on plant is provided at 5% per annum on the original cost.
- *Payments for expenses:* In the previous year all operating expenses were paid in the month in which they occurred. However, in the budget year the procedure will be two-thirds of the selling expenses will be paid in the month in which they are incurred with the balance being paid in the following month; and administrative expenses will continue to be paid in the month in which they are incurred.

Required

Prepare a cash budget for each of the first three months of the budget year showing the estimated cash in hand at the end of each month.

4.13 Using the following information from the Shamash Company prepare a cash budget for the months of October, November and December.

Estimated figures

	August $	September $	October $	November $	December $
Cash sales	230 000	250 000	160 000	200 000	240 000
Credit sales	256 000	276 000	188 000	228 000	264 000
Cash purchases	90 000	84 000	176 000	220 000	84 000
Credit purchases	220 000	60 000	160 000	228 000	200 000
Weeks in the month	4	5	4	4	5

	$	$
Rent paid per week		800
Rent received per week		200
Wages per week		
Selling	13 600	
Administration	3 600	
Distribution	17 200	34 400
Other operating expenses per week		
Selling	3 600	
Administration	1 000	
Distribution	3 200	7 800

- Accounts receivable regularly settle their accounts as follows: 85% pay in the month following sale — these accounts take advantage of a 5% discount; 10% pay in the second month; 3% pay in the third month; the balance is written off as bad.
- July accounts were paid in full in September.
- Accounts payable are settled in the month following purchase and 85% allowed a discount benefit of 5%.
- The other operating expenses include an amount of $1600 per month for depreciation as follows:

	$
Selling	600
Administration	400
Distribution	600

- Bank balance as at 30 September was $55 670.

4.14 The following information gives particulars of actual results for November and December and budgeted results for January to March for the business of Tane Emporium.

Month	Sales			Non-current acquisitions	
	Credit	Cash	Total	Units	
	$	$	$		$
November	126 000	14 000	140 000	14 000	—
December	113 400	12 600	126 000	12 600	21 000
January	119 700	13 300	133 000	13 300	—
February	138 600	15 400	154 000	15 400	—
March	151 200	16 800	168 000	16 800	25 200
April	126 000	14 000	140 000	14 000	—

- Credit sales are invoiced on the last day of the month. Of the credit sales, it is found that 80% pay their accounts within one month of the invoice date, and a further 15% pay during the second month after invoice date. The balance is found to be irrecoverable.

- Inventory, at the end of each month, has been and is required to be 20% of the quantity that is expected to be sold in the following month. The purchase price for each unit of inventory is $6, and is not expected to change. Purchases of inventory are paid for 20% in the month of purchase and 80% in the following month.
- Selling and administrative expenses, including a depreciation charge of $2800, are incurred at the rate of $16 800 per month. Payment is made in the month following the month in which the expense is incurred.
- Tane Emporium also has to service a loan of $280 000. Interest at the rate of 12% per annum is payable quarterly, the next due dates being 31 December and 31 March. No repayment of principal is required during the budget period.
- The balance of the bank account at 31 December is $8400.

Required

Prepare a cash budget for the months of January, February and March.

4.15 Chiron Book Distributors provides you with the following figures:

	$
June sales (actual)	28 000
July sales (budgeted)	26 000
August sales (budgeted)	24 000
September sales (budgeted)	16 800

- Sales are expected to be 70% credit and 30% cash. Invoices for credit sales are issued at the end of each month. Accounts receivable pay: 70% within 30 days of invoice receiving 5% discount; 20% within 60 days; 5% within 90 days; 5% bad debts.
- Accounts receivable balances as at 30 June are $31 600, made up of April sales $2400, May sales $9600 and June sales $19 600.
- Purchases are paid for in the month in which they are made. Budgeted purchases are:

	$
July	16 000
August	15 200
September	8 000

- Marketing expenses are budgeted at 10% of sales and are paid in the month in which they are incurred.
- Other expenses are expected to be:

	$
July	6 000
August	4 800
September	7 200

- Other expenses are paid in the same month that they are incurred.
- Depreciation is included in the other expenses above and is $2000 per month.
- Machinery will be paid for on 20 August for $20 000.
- Cash balance at the end of June is $32 000.

Required

Prepare a cash budget for July, August and September.

4.16 The following information pertains to Carnabon Industries:

- Balance of cash at bank 1 November — $27 000.
- Actual sales for September and October and estimated sales for November are:

	September $	October $	November $
Cash sales	19 500	15 750	22 200
Credit sales	60 000	90 000	120 000
	79 500	105 750	142 200

- Collections from accounts receivable follow a pattern: 15% in month of sale; 60% in month following sale; 20% in second month after sale; 5% are uncollectable.
- Purchases for November are expected to be $75 000 — 25% of a month's purchases are paid for in the month of purchase. Accounts payable at 31 October of $48 000 will be paid in November.
- Selling and administration expenses for November are expected to be $39 000. Of this amount, $12 000 is for depreciation.
- Equipment costing $54 000 will be purchased for cash during November. The proprietor will make cash drawings of $9000 in the same month.
- It is desired that Carnabon Industries maintain a minimum cash balance of $15 000. Any shortfall will need to be financed by borrowings.

Required

Prepare a cash budget for the month of November. Indicate in the financing section any borrowings, if required.

4.17 Rhegium Realty is a large real estate agency. It had a cash balance of $8300 at 1 April. Rhegium expects that receipt of commissions will be $75 000 in April and $101 500 in May. The business should receive investment income of $33 300 in May. Projected cash payments are $110 000 in April and $125 800 in May. Due to special financing arrangements, a minimum cash balance of $6000 is required by the firm's bank. When the bank account balance drops below $6000 the bank credits the account, by way of a loan, with the amount needed to make up the shortfall, but only in multiples of $500. Rhegium borrows as little as possible and repays the loan, again in multiples of $500, as quickly as possible. Interest is paid monthly on the entire outstanding balance (as it stands immediately before any repayments) at the rate of 12% per annum.

Required

Prepare a cash budget for the two months April and May.

4.18 Central Medical Centre provides a wide range of hospital services in its community. The hospital's board of directors has recently authorised the following capital expenditures:

	$
Neonatal care equipment	900 000
CT scanner	800 000
X-ray equipment	650 000
Laboratory equipment	1 450 000
Total	3 800 000

The expenditures are planned for 1 October, and the board wishes to know the amount of borrowing, if any, necessary on that date. Marc Kelly, chief accountant, has gathered the following information to be used in preparing an analysis of future cash flows.

• Billings, made in the month of service, for the first six months of the year are:

Month	Actual amount
	$
January	4 400 000
February	4 400 000
March	4 500 000
April	4 500 000
May	5 000 000
June	5 000 000

• Ninety per cent of the hospital's billings are made to third parties: Medicare, federal or state governments, and private insurance companies. The remaining 10% of the billings are made directly to the patients. Historical patterns of billing collections are:

	Third party billings %	Direct patient billings %
During month of service	20	10
During month following service	50	40
During second month after service	20	40
Uncollectable	10	10

- Estimated billings for the last six months of the year under review are listed below. The same billing and collection patterns that have been experienced during the first six months of the year are expected to continue during the last six months of the year.

Month	Estimated amount $
July	4 500 000
August	5 000 000
September	5 500 000
October	5 700 000
November	5 800 000
December	5 500 000

- The purchases of the previous three months and the planned purchases for the last six months of the year are presented in the following schedule.

Month	Amount $
April	1 100 000
May	1 200 000
June	1 200 000
July	1 250 000
August	1 500 000
September	1 850 000
October	1 950 000
November	2 250 000
December	1 750 000

- Endowment fund income is expected to continue at the rate of $175 000 per month.
- The hospital has a cash balance of $300 000 on 1 July and has a policy maintaining a minimum end-of-month cash balance of 10% of the current month's purchases.
- All purchases are made on account and accounts payable are paid in the month following the purchase.
- Salaries for each month during July to December are expected to be $1 500 000 plus 20% of that month's billings. Salaries are paid in the month of service.
- The hospital's monthly depreciation charges are $125 000.
- The medical centre incurs interest expenses of $150 000 per month and makes interest payments of $450 000 on the last day of each quarter (that is, 31 March, 30 June, 30 September and 31 December).

Required
(a) Prepare a schedule of budgeted cash receipts by month for the third quarter of the year (July through to September).

(b) Prepare a schedule of budgeted cash disbursements by month for the third quarter of the year.

(c) Determine the amount of borrowing, if any, necessary on 1 October to acquire the capital items totalling $3 800 000.[1]

4.19 Tegea Traders make all their sales on credit. Budgeted sales are:

	Units
July	10 000
August	11 000
September	12 000
October	12 500

- Selling price is $7 per unit.
- Collections are expected to be 60% in the month of sale and 38% in the next month. It is anticipated that the remainder will be uncollectable.
- Accounts receivable balance at 30 June is $26 600, which will be received in July.
- Purchases are equal to 70% of the projected sales dollars for the following month. Purchases are paid in full in the month after purchase.
- Selling and distribution expenses are paid for each month and are expected to be $11 550 per month.
- Additionally, depreciation is $3500 each month.
- Cash balance at 1 July is $5600.

Required

For the quarter ending 30 September prepare:

(a) sales budget
(b) purchases budget
(c) schedule of collections from accounts receivable
(d) schedule of payments for purchases
(e) cash budget.

Endnote

1 Hilton, R., *Managerial Accounting*, 2nd edn, New York, USA: McGraw-Hill Book Company, 1994

Chapter 5

Budgeted financial statements for service organisations

Introduction

Financial statements are reports which disclose the results and financial position of an enterprise. They are usually comprised of the revenue statement (or profit and loss statement), the balance sheet and the statement of cash flows.

Budgeted financial statements are the capstone of the master budget and summarise the forecasts made in all other budgets.

This chapter will deal with the preparation of the:

* budgeted revenue statement
* budgeted balance sheet
* budgeted cash flows statement.

Budgeted revenue statements revisited

Chapter 3 introduced budgeted revenue statements. Recall that these statements can be prepared in summary format, showing only category totals, or detailed format, showing individual items appropriately classified. Management will decide which format is appropriate for different circumstances or levels in the organisational hierarchy.

A budgeted revenue statement discloses the forecast profit or loss for the budgeted period. Management is then able to change plans and amend budgets if the budgeted results are unsatisfactory. When management is satisfied with the budgets, they can be used for monitoring and control purposes (see Chapter 7).

A summary budgeted revenue statement is reproduced below.

Tough as Teak

Budgeted revenue statement for the 3 months ending 30 June

	April $	May $	June $	Quarter $
Sales	43 000	38 000	41 000	122 000
less **Cost of goods sold**	21 500	19 000	20 500	61 000
Gross profit	21 500	19 000	20 500	61 000
less **Operating expenses**				
Marketing expenses	6 716	6 331	6 562	19 609
Administration expenses	2 300	2 300	2 300	6 900
Financial expenses	640	627	613	1 880
Total operating expenses	9 656	9 258	9 475	28 389
Net profit	11 844	9 742	11 025	32 611

Self-test problem 5.1

Sales and operating expenses budgets for Ammon Artefacts, for the three months ending 30 September appear below.

Ammon Artefacts

Sales budget for the quarter ending 30 September

	$
July	22 000
August	23 000
September	23 500
	68 500

Ammon Artefacts

Cost of goods sold budget for the quarter ending 30 September

	July $	August $	September $	Quarter $
Beginning inventory	22 000	23 000	23 500	22 000
Purchases	16 200	16 960	17 490	50 650
Goods available for sale	38 200	39 960	40 990	72 650
less Ending inventory	23 000	23 500	24 400	24 400
Cost of goods sold	15 200	16 460	16 590	48 250

Ammon Artefacts

Marketing expenses budget for the quarter ending 30 September

	July $	August $	September $	Quarter $
Sales commissions	1 100	1 150	1 175	3 425
Depreciation:				
Shop fittings	600	600	600	1 800
Total marketing expenses	1 700	1 750	1 775	5 225

Ammon Artefacts

Administration expenses budget for the quarter ending 30 September

	July $	August $	September $	Quarter $
Telephone and stationery	175	175	175	525
Rent	1 600	1 600	1 600	4 800
Depreciation:				
Motor vehicles	500	500	500	1 500
Office equipment	190	190	190	570
Total administration expenses	2 465	2 465	2 465	7 395

Ammon Artefacts

Financial expenses budget
for the quarter ending 30 September

	July $	August $	September $	Quarter $
Bad debts	220	230	235	685
Bank charges etc	60	60	60	180
Total financial expenses	280	290	295	865

Required
Prepare a detailed revenue statement for the three months ending 30 September.
Show each month.

For small organisations, individual operating budgets may not be necessary. A cash budget and budgeted financial statements may be all that are required. In these circumstances it is possible to start with a previous period's figures and adjust these by forecasting changes for the coming budget period. It must be stressed that this is only appropriate for simple situations.

Consider Hambly and Hyde, a firm of accountants in Albany, Western Australia. Figures for the last financial year were:

	$
Fees income	350 000
Professional labour	140 000
Support labour	60 000
Stationery	5 000
Travel	10 000
Phones/faxes	2 000
Photocopying	1 000
Rent	12 000
Depreciation	4 000

Anticipated changes for the forthcoming financial year include:

- fees income should increase by 6%
- labour charges are expected to increase by 10%
- stationery, phones/faxes and photocopying are all anticipated to increase by 5%
- travel should decrease by 8%.

Rent and depreciation are predicted to remain unchanged.

Hambly and Hyde's budgeted revenue statement, with calculations in brackets, appears below.

Hambly and Hyde

Budgeted revenue statement for the year ending 30 June

		$	$
Fees income	($350 000 × 1.06)		371 000
less Expenses			253 600
Professional labour	($140 000 × 1.1)	154 000	
Support labour	($60 000 × 1.1)	66 000	
Stationery	($5 000 × 1.05)	5 250	
Travel	($10 000 × 0.92)	9 200	
Phones/faxes	($2 000 × 1.05)	2 100	
Photocopying	($1 000 × 1.05)	1 050	
Rent		12 000	
Depreciation		4 000	
Net profit			117 400

Self-test problem 5.2

A. Green and Associates are architectural engineers. Actual results for last year were:

	$
Fees income	623 700
Advertising	12 480
Accounting fees	6 650
Draught persons' salaries	217 700
Contract draught person	25 480
Travelling	36 000
Rent	24 000
Printing of plans	6 230
Office salaries	98 000
Subscriptions to professional association	1 800
Telephone and stationery	3 990
Motor vehicle expenses	7 000
Bad debts	6 240
Bank charges etc	2 360
Interest expense	15 000

- Fees income is estimated to increase by 4%.
- Advertising will be 2% of fees income.
- Bad debts are estimated to be 1% of fees income.
- Rent will increase by 10%.
- Interest expense will decrease by 15%.
- All other expenses are expected to increase by 5%.

Required
Prepare a budgeted revenue statement for the coming year ending 30 June.

You should now be able to do Question 5.1

Preparing budgeted financial statements

Electronique, a retailer of electrical appliances located in Darwin, will be used to illustrate the preparation of budgeted financial statements throughout the rest of this chapter.

Budgets which Electronique need to prepare are shown in Figure 5.1.

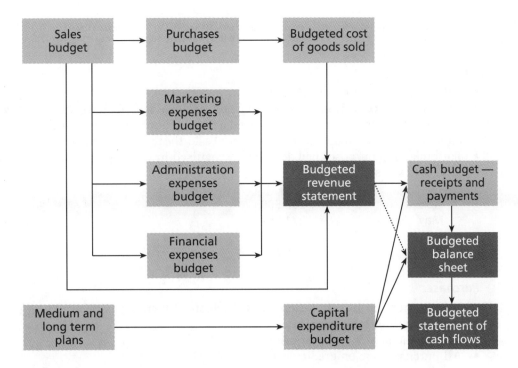

Figure 5.1 *Master budget for Electronique — budgeted financial statements highlighted*

Marcus Evans, Electronique's accountant, is preparing the budgets for the quarter ending 30 June. He has established the following information.

Trial balance at 31 March

	$	$
Delivery vehicle	24 000	
Accumulated depreciation — delivery vehicle		9 600
Shop fittings	28 000	
Accumulated depreciation — shop fittings		12 600
Office furniture and equipment	16 000	
Accumulated depreciation — office furniture and equipment		7 200
Investments	360 000	
Bank	15 000	
Accounts receivable*	160 000	
Inventory	80 250	
Accounts payable		70 000
Capital		583 850
	683 250	683 250

* Accounts receivable are made up of: February sales of $40 000 to be collected in April;
  March sales of $120 000 to be collected — $75 000 in April and $45 000 in May

Sales

- All sales are made on credit.
- The pattern of collections from accounts receivable is anticipated to be: 50% pay in the same month — these are allowed a 5% discount; 30% pay in the month after sale; 18% pay in the second month after sale; the remainder are uncollectable.
- For budgeting purposes bad debts are recognised in the month of sale.
- Expected sales are:

	$
April	262 500
May	271 250
June	280 000
July	288 750

Purchases

- Management desires that each month's closing inventory is to be 50% of the following month's cost of sales.
- Sales value is 175% of cost price.
- All purchases are on credit.
- Purchases are paid for 40% in the month of purchase and 60% in the following month.

Other income and expenditure

- Expenses are paid in the month in which they are incurred.
- Marketing expenses paid are 20% of sales for the month.

- Administration expenses paid are 10% of sales for the month.
- Monthly interest of $3000 is received in respect of the investment.

Depreciation

- Delivery vehicle is 20% per annum on cost.
- Shop fittings is 15% per annum on cost.
- Office furniture and equipment is 15% per annum on cost.

Additional information

- The owner of Electronique will take cash drawings of $3000 each month.
- New office equipment will be purchased on 27 June for $5000.

Tag the above information for easy reference

Budgeted revenue statements

After preparing the sales budget and operating expense budgets, Marcus Evans produced the budgeted revenue statement shown below. Explanations appear after the statement.

Electronique

Budgeted revenue statement for the 3 months ending 30 June

	April $	May $	June $	Quarter $
Sales	262 500	271 250	280 000	813 750
less **Cost of goods sold**				
Beginning inventory	80 250	77 500	80 000	80 250
Purchases[a]	147 250	157 500	162 500	467 250
Goods available for sale	227 500	235 000	242 500	547 500
less Ending inventory	77 500	80 000	82 500	82 500
Cost of goods sold	150 000	155 000	160 000	465 000
Gross profit	112 500	116 250	120 000	348 750
add Interest income	3 000	3 000	3 000	9 000
Operating income	115 500	119 250	123 000	357 750
less **Operating expenses**				
Marketing expenses				
In cash[b]	52 500	54 250	56 000	162 750
Depreciation[c]	750	750	750	2 250
	53 250	55 000	56 750	165 000

(financial statement continued on next page)

(continued from previous page)

	April $	May $	June $	Quarter $
Administration expenses				
In cash[d]	26 250	27 125	28 000	81 375
Depreciation[e]	200	200	200	600
	26 450	27 325	28 200	81 975
Financial expenses				
Bad debts[f]	5 250	5 425	5 600	16 275
Discount allowed[g]	6 563	6 781	7 000	20 344
	11 813	12 206	12 600	36 619
Total operating expenses	91 513	94 531	97 550	283 594
Net profit	23 987	24 719	25 450	74 156

(a) Purchases

	April $	May $	June $	Quarter $
Cost of sales (100/175 × sales)	150 000	155 000	160 000	465 000
add Ending inventory	77 500	80 000	82 500	82 500
Total requirements	227 500	235 000	242 500	547 500
less Beginning inventory	80 250	77 500	80 000	80 250
To be purchased	147 250	157 500	162 500	467 250

(b) Marketing expenses — in cash

		$
April	(20% × $262 500)	52 500
May	(20% × $271 250)	54 250
June	(20% × $280 000)	56 000
		162 750

(c) Depreciation

Delivery vehicle:
Per annum   20% × $24 000 = $4800
Per month $4800/12 = $400
Shop fittings:
Per annum   15% × $28 000 = $4200
Per month $4200/12 = $350

(d) Administration expenses — in cash

		$
April	(10% × $262 500)	26 250
May	(10% × $271 250)	27 125
June	(10% × $280 000)	28 000
		81 375

(e) Depreciation

As the new office equipment (costing $5000) will not be purchased until the end of the budget year, it will not incur depreciation in this period.

Per annum	15% × $16 000 = $2400
Per month	$2400/12 = $200

(f) Financial expenses — bad debts

		$
April	(2% × $262 500)	5 250
May	(2% × $271 250)	5 425
June	(2% × $280 000)	5 600
		16 275

(g) Discount allowed

		$
April	(50% × $262 500 × 5%)	6 563
May	(50% × $271 250 × 5%)	6 781
June	(50% × $280 000 × 5%)	7 000
		20 344

Self-test problem 5.3

Gaea Gallery is preparing its budgets for the quarter ending 31 March. The following data is relevant:

- Forecast sales are:

	$
January	25 000
February	30 000
March	35 000

- Forty per cent of all sales are on credit. Estimated collections are: 50% in the month of sale, with a discount of 3%; 30% in the month after sale; 15% in the second month after sale; the remainder are uncollectable.
- For budgeting purposes bad debts are recognised in the month of sale.
- Cash sales receive a 5% discount.
- Purchases, all on credit, are estimated at 75% of sales each month — 80% of purchases are paid in the month of purchase and a 2% discount is received; 20% of purchases are paid in the month following purchase.
- Estimated expenses per month are: marketing — $1000; administration — $2000.
- Depreciation on equipment, included in the administration expense above, is $375 per month.
- It is anticipated that inventory on hand at 31 March will be valued at $15 000.
- A mortgage repayment of $3000 is due in February.
- The balance sheet for Gaea Gallery is shown below:

Gaea Gallery

Balance sheet as at 31 December

	$	$
Proprietor's funds		25 650
Represented by:		
Current assets		26 150
Bank	5 000	
Accounts receivable	9 150	
Inventory	12 000	
Current liability		6 000
Accounts payable	6 000	
Working capital		20 150
Non-current assets		17 500
Equipment	30 000	
Accumulated depreciation	12 500	
		37 650
Non-current liability		12 000
Mortgage	12 000	
Net assets		25 650

- Accounts receivable at 31 December are all collectable. Estimated collections are: January — $6750, February — $2400.

Required
Prepare a budgeted revenue statement for the quarter ending 31 March. Prepare the budget for the quarter in total, not month by month.

You should now be able to do Questions 5.2 to 5.6

Budgeted balance sheets

After preparing the budgeted revenue statement, Marcus Evans produced Electronique's budgeted balance sheet as shown below. Explanations are given after the balance sheet.

Electronique

Budgeted balance sheet as at 30 June

	$	$	$
Proprietor's funds			
Capital 1 April			583 850
add Net profit			74 156
			658 006
less Drawings			9 000
Total proprietor's funds			649 006
Represented by:			
Current assets			345 756
Bank[a]		80 031	
Accounts receivable[b]		183 225	
Inventory		82 500	
Current liability			97 500
Accounts payable[c]		97 500	
Working capital			248 256
Non-current assets			400 750
Delivery vehicle	24 000		
less Accumulated depreciation[d]	10 800	13 200	
Shop fittings	28 000		
less Accumulated depreciation[d]	13 650	14 350	
Office furniture and equipment	21 000		
less Accumulated depreciation[d]	7 800	13 200	
Investments		360 000	
Net assets			649 006

(a) Bank balance

The balance for the bank account was found from the cash budget which is reproduced below. This budget was prepared by following the procedure illustrated in Chapter 4.

Electronique

Cash budget for the quarter ending 30 June

	April $	May $	June $
Beginning cash balance — surplus	15 000	47 037	66 906
Receipts			
Accounts receivable*	239 687	252 594	261 625
Interest from investments	3 000	3 000	3 000
Total receipts	242 687	255 594	264 625
Cash available for needs	257 687	302 631	331 531
Payments			
Accounts payable†	128 900	151 350	159 500
Marketing expenses (20% of sales)	52 500	54 250	56 000
Administration expenses (10% of sales)	26 250	27 125	28 000
Drawings	3 000	3 000	3 000
Purchase office equipment			5 000
Total payments	210 650	235 725	251 500
Closing cash balance — surplus	47 037	66 906	80 031

- Collections from accounts receivable:*

		Month of receipt		
Month of sale	**Workings**	**April $**	**May $**	**June $**
February	given	40 000		
March	given	75 000	45 000	
April	50% × $262 500 × 95%	124 687		
	30% × $262 500		78 750	
	18% × $262 500			47 250
May	50% × $271 250 × 95%		128 844	
	30% × $271 250			81 375
June	50% × $280 000 × 95%			133 000
Total collections		239 687	252 594	261 625

- Payments to accounts payable:†

		Month paid		
Month of purchase		**April $**	**May $**	**June $**
March	given	70 000		
April	$147 250	(40%) 58 900	(60%) 88 350	
May	$157 500		(40%) 63 000	(60%) 94 500
June	$162 500			(40%) 65 000
Total payments		128 900	151 350	159 500

(b) Accounts receivable balance

		$
From May sales	(18% × $271 250)	48 825
From June sales	(48% × $280 000)	134 400
		183 225

(c) Accounts payable balance:

		$
From June purchases	(60% × $162 500)	97 500

(d) Accumulated depreciation balances

		$
Delivery vehicle	($400 × 3 + $9600)	10 800
Shop fittings	($350 × 3 + $12 600)	13 650
Office furniture and equipment	($200 × 3 + $7200)	7 800

Self-test problem 5.4

Refer to Self-test problem 5.3.

Required
Prepare Gaea Gallery's budgeted balance sheet as at 31 March. *Hint:* You will need to prepare a cash budget to find the closing bank balance.

You should now be able to do Questions 5.7 to 5.9

Budgeted statements of cash flows

Cash budgets present the forecast cash receipts and payments, and changes in cash balances. Budgeted statements of cash flows effectively serve the same purpose, but they are presented in a format which complies with the requirements of accounting standards AAS 28 and AASB 1026, both entitled, *Statement of Cash Flows*.

Format of statement of cash flows

Figure 5.2 shows a pro forma presentation of a statement of cash flows for a sole trader or partnership. Cash outflows are shown in rounded brackets and cash inflows without brackets.

[Name of organisation]
Budgeted statement of cash flows
for the period ended ...

	$	$
Cash flows from operating activities		
Inflows:		
Collections from customers		XXXX
Interest received		XXXX
Dividends from investments		XXXX
		XXXX
Outflows:		
Payments to employees	(XXXX)	
Payments to suppliers	(XXXX)	
Interest paid	(XXXX)	(XXXX)
Net cash inflow/(outflow) from operating activities		XXXX
Cash flows from investing activities		
Acquisition of non-current assets	(XXXX)	
Proceeds from sale of non-current assets	XXXX	
Net cash inflow/(outflow) from investing activities		XXXX
Cash flows from financing activities		
New capital introduced	XXXX	
Proceeds from borrowings	XXXX	
Repayment of borrowings	(XXXX)	
Drawings	(XXXX)	
Net cash inflow/(outflow) from financing activities		XXXX
Net increase/(decrease) in cash held		XXXX
Cash at beginning of period		XXXX
Cash at end of period		XXXX

Figure 5.2 *Pro forma statement of cash flows*

It can be seen that the cash flow statement is divided into three main activities: operating; investing; and financing. AAS 28 defines these as follows:

- **Operating activities:** Those activities which relate to the provision of goods and services. They also include interest and dividends received and interest paid.
- **Investing activities:** Those activities which relate to the acquisition and disposal of non-current assets, including property, plant and equipment and other productive assets, and investments, such as securities.

- **Financing activities:** Those activities which relate to changing the size and composition of the financial structure of the entity, including equity.

The overriding consideration is whether the activity affects bank accounts, cash on hand or petty cash.

Preparation of budgeted statements of cash flows

Marcus Evans has produced the Electronique's budgeted statement of cash flows. It appears below. Explanations follow the statement.

Electronique

Budgeted statement of cash flows
for the quarter ending 30 June

	$	$
Cash flows from operating activities		
Inflows:		
Collections from customers[a]		753 906
Interest from investments[b]		9 000
		762 906
Outflows:		
Payments to employees[c]	(120 000)	
Payments to suppliers[d]	(563 875)	(683 875)
Net cash inflow from operating activities		79 031
Cash flows from investing activities		
Purchase of office equipment	(5 000)	
Net cash outflow from investing activities		(5 000)
Cash flows from financing activities		
Drawings[e]	(9 000)	
Net cash outflow from financing activities		(9 000)
Net increase in cash held		65 031
Cash balance 1 July		15 000
Cash balance 30 June		80 031

(a) Collections

From collections from accounts receivable schedule:

	$
April	239 687
May	252 594
June	261 625
	753 906

(b) Interest

Interest from investments is $3000 per month for 3 months ($9000).

(c) Payments to employees

Marcus established that wages, salaries, commissions, etc paid to employees totalled $40 000 per month. Wages were included in marketing and administration expenses ($40 000 × 3 = $120 000).

(d) Payments to suppliers

Payments to suppliers means payments for all goods and services other than employees. This figure was calculated as follows:

	April $	May $	June $	Quarter $
From payments to accounts payable schedule	128 900	151 350	159 500	439 750
Marketing expense payments	52 500	54 250	56 000	162 750
Administration expense payments	26 250	27 125	28 000	81 375
	207 650	232 725	243 500	683 875
less Payments to employees	40 000	40 000	40 000	120 000
Payments to suppliers	167 650	192 725	203 500	563 875

Note that it is also acceptable to disclose payments to suppliers for goods separate from payments to others for services. If this approach is adopted then, instead of 'Payments to suppliers (563 875)', that part of the cash flow statement would appear as:

	$	$
Outflows:		
Payment to employees	(120 000)	
Payment to suppliers for goods	(439 750)	
Payments to others for services	(124 125)	(683 875)

(e) Drawings

Drawings are $3000 per month for 3 months ($9000).

Self-test problem 5.5

Refer to Self-test problem 5.3. Gaea Gallery is managed by a semi-retired person who is paid $1000 per month, which is split evenly between marketing and administration expenses. All other workers are volunteers.

Required
Prepare a budgeted cash flow statement for the quarter ending 31 March.

You should now be able to do Questions 5.10 to 5.12

Integration of budgets

As has been shown, individual budgets are of limited usefulness. All budgets are interrelated and together make up the master budget. You will recall that a master budget is a combination of all the budgets of an organisation, dealing with all phases of the operations of the business for a particular period of time.

You should now be able to do Questions 5.13 to 5.17

Checklist

Before progressing to the next chapter, complete the checklist below. This will identify whether you have an understanding of the important parts of the chapter.

Can you do the following?

❏ Prepare budgeted revenue statements for merchandising firms and other service organisations
❏ Prepare budgeted balance sheets for merchandising firms and other service organisations
❏ Compile budgeted statements of cash flows
❏ Prepare master budgets for merchandising firms and other service organisations

Questions

5.1 A. D. Vocate, a solicitor in Bendigo, Victoria, estimates the following in relation to her practice:

Fees income	October — $20 000 November — $25 000 December — $18 000
Professional labour	$120 000 pa apportioned equally each month
Support labour	$60 000 pa apportioned equally each month
Advertising	1% of fees income
Stationery and photocopying	$4200 pa apportioned equally each month
Travel	5% of fees income
Rent	$800 per month
Depreciation	$3000 pa apportioned equally each month
Phones/faxes	$1200 pa apportioned equally each month
Bank charges etc	$600 pa apportioned equally each month

Required

Prepare a budgeted revenue statement, month by month, for the three months ending 31 December.

5.2 Takami Transport Corporation anticipates haulage fees for May will be $490 000. Bad debts are expected to be 2% of sales and will be recognised in the month of sale. Gross profit should be 35% of gross fees. Takami Transport has also provided the following additional information for the budget month of May:

- fixed marketing expenses — $9700
- variable marketing expenses — 10% of sales
- fixed administration expenses — $30 000
- variable administration expenses — 5% of sales.

Required

Prepare a budgeted revenue statement for May.

5.3 Etana Enterprises anticipates the following will occur in February:
- Sales are expected to be $280 000.
- Bad debts are estimated to be 2.5% of sales. They are recognised in the month of sale for budgeting purposes.
- Inventory is $63 000 at the start of February. It is expected to increase by $9000 by the end of the month.
- Goods are sold with a 40% mark up on cost.
- Expenses are expected to be: marketing — $17 500; administration — $23 000.

Required

Prepare the budgeted revenue statement for the month of February.

5.4 Consus Nurseries provides information relevant to the preparation of budgets for the three months ending 30 September.

Sales	$
July	187 200
August	243 600
September	259 200

- Gross profit is 30% of cost price.

Inventory	$
30 June (actual)	30 780
31 July	36 240
31 August	39 300
30 September	24 000

- Operating expenses (expected payments): marketing — 8% of sales; administration — 7% of sales; finance — $1200 per month.

Balance day adjustments

	Accruals $	Prepayments $
30 June (actual):		
Marketing	200	—
Administration	1 000	160
31 July:		
Marketing	400	—
Administration	900	580
31 August:		
Marketing	250	—
Administration	820	530
30 September:		
Marketing	100	—
Administration	400	200

Required

Prepare a budgeted revenue statement, month by month, for the quarter ending 30 September. Be sure to show the detail for cost of goods sold.

5.5 The Mason Agency, a division of General Service Industries, offers consulting services to clients for a fee. The corporate management at General Service is pleased with the performance of the Mason Agency for the first nine months of the current year and has recommended that the division manager of Mason Agency, Richard Howell, submit a revised forecast for the remaining quarter, as the division has exceeded the annual plan year-to-date by 20% of operating income. An unexpected increase in billed hour volume over the original plan is the main reason for this increase in income. The original operating budget for the first three quarters for Mason Agency follows.

The Mason Agency

Operating budget

	1st quarter	2nd quarter	3rd quarter	Total for 9 months
	$	$	$	$
Revenue				
Consulting fees:				
Management consulting	315 000	315 000	315 000	945 000
Computer system consulting	421 875	421 875	421 875	1 265 625
Total consulting revenue	736 875	736 875	736 875	2 210 625
Other revenue	10 000	10 000	10 000	30 000
	746 875	746 875	746 875	2 240 625
Expenses				
Consultant salary expenses	386 750	386 750	386 750	1 160 250
Travel and related expenses	45 625	45 625	45 625	136 875
General and administration expenses	100 000	100 000	100 000	300 000
Depreciation expense	40 000	40 000	40 000	120 000
Corporate expense allocation	50 000	50 000	50 000	150 000
Total expenses	622 375	622 375	622 375	1 867 125
Operating income	124 500	124 500	124 500	373 500

Richard will reflect the following information in his revised forecast for the fourth quarter:

- The division currently has 25 consultants on staff, 10 for management consulting and 15 for computer systems consulting. Three additional management consultants have been hired to start work at the beginning of the fourth quarter to meet the increased client demand.
- The hourly billing rate for consulting revenue will remain at $90 per hour for each management consultant and $75 per hour for each computer consultant. However, due to the favourable increase in billing hour volume when compared to the plan, the hours for each consultant will be increased by 50 per quarter.
- The budgeted annual salaries and actual annual salaries, paid monthly, are the same: $50 000 for a management consultant and $46 000 for a computer consultant. Corporate management has approved a merit increase of 10% at the beginning of the fourth quarter for all 25 existing consultants, while the new consultants will be compensated at the planned rate.
- The planned salary expense includes a provision for employee fringe benefits amounting to 30% of the annual salaries. However, the improvement of some corporate-wide employee programs will increase the fringe benefits to 40%.
- The original plan assumes a fixed hourly rate for travel and other related expenses for each billing hour of consulting. These are expenses that are not reimbursed by the client, and the previously determined hourly rate has proved to be adequate to cover these costs.
- Other revenue is derived from temporary rentals and interest income and remains unchanged for the fourth quarter.
- General and administrative expenses have been favourable at 7% below the plan. This 7% savings on fourth quarter expenses will be reflected in the revised plan.
- Depreciation of office equipment and personal computers will stay constant at the projected straight-line rate.
- Due to the favourable experience for the first three quarters, and the division's increased ability to absorb costs, the corporate management at General Service Industries has increased the corporate expense allocation by 50%.

Required

(a) Prepare a revised operating budget for the fourth quarter for the Mason Agency that Richard Howell will present to General Services Industries.
(b) Discuss the reasons why an organisation would prepare a revised operating budget.[1]

5.6 Khumbaba Wholesalers' selling price is 140% of cost. Beginning inventory must be 154% of that month's cost of sales.

Estimated sales

	$
January	178 500
February	166 250
March	192 500
April	175 000

- Marketing expenses have a fixed element of $15 750 per month.
- Variable marketing expenses are 5% of sales.
- Administration expenses are $21 500 per month.
- Lease payment of $21 000 is due in February — to be treated as a financial expense.
- Mortgage interest of $3500 is due in March.

Required

Prepare the budgeted revenue statement for the three months ending 31 March.

5.7 The post-closing trial balance of Jim Amphion, a part time landscape gardener, for last year discloses:

	$	$
Inventories of materials	7 800	
Accounts receivable	5 300	
Bank	8 200	
Equipment	7 600	
Accumulated depreciation		
— equipment		2 850
Motor vehicle	21 000	
Accumulated depreciation		
— motor vehicle		10 500
Long term loan		10 000
Accounts payable		3 200
Capital		23 350
	49 900	49 900

- Net profit is expected to be $15 000.
- Accounts payable will increase by 10%.
- Accounts receivable will increase by 10%.
- Inventories will decrease by 5%.

- Depreciation on equipment is 15% per annum on cost.
- Depreciation on motor vehicle is 20% per annum on cost.
- Drawings are anticipated at $10 000.
- $3000 will be paid off the long term loan.
- Bank will be the balancing figure.

Required

Prepare the budgeted balance sheet as at 30 June next year.

5.8 Yarilo Health Products provide you with the following information relating to the month of April.

Beginning bank balance	$13 200
Budgeted sales	$204 600
Cost of goods sold	50% of sales
Ending accounts receivable balance	25% of the month's sales
Cash receipts	$255 750
Ending inventory balance	$148 500
Cash payments for inventories and accounts payable	$198 000
Cash purchases of fixed assets	$19 800
Ending accounts payable balance	$80 850
1 April balances	Fixed assets — $574 200 Accumulated depreciation — $457 050
Depreciation for April	$4950
April operating expenses	Expected to be $69 300 — half is paid in April, the remainder will be accrued at 30 April
Beginning capital balance	$204 600

Required

Prepare the budgeted balance sheet as at 30 April.

5.9   Westvale Provision Centre is one of several businesses owned by Juanita
Searle.

Westvale Provision Centre

Budgeted balance sheet as at 30 June, Year 1

	$	$
Proprietor's funds		
Capital — J. Searle		63 000
Represented by:		
Current assets		37 800
Bank	3 000	
Accounts receivable	24 000	
Inventory	10 800	
Current liability		30 000
Accounts payable	18 000	
Mortgage loan	12 000	
Working capital		7 800
Non-current assets		55 200
Land (at cost)	12 000	
Buildings (at cost)	21 000	
Plant (net)	14 400	
Motor vehicle (net)	3 600	
Investments	4 200	
Net assets		63 000

Juanita anticipates that the following events will occur in Year 2:

- Additions to buildings will amount to $12 000.
- Plant will be sold for $3000. This plant has a written down value of
  $4800 at time of sale. Purchase of new plant for $6000 will take
  place.
- Sale of all the investments at a loss of $600.
- Bank account to increase by $3300.
- Accounts receivable to increase to $30 000.
- Inventory to increase by 50%.
- Additional capital of $6000 to be contributed.
- Current mortgage to be paid off.
- Provision for depreciation on plant of $3600 and on motor vehicle
  of $600.
- Accounts payable to increase to $21 000.

- The net profit after depreciation, but before taking into account gain or loss on disposal of non-current assets, is expected to be $18 000.
- A new mortgage, repayable in two years, will be taken out.

Required

Prepare the budgeted balance sheet as at 30 June, Year 2. *Hint:* The new mortgage is the balancing figure.

5.10 Doris Lloyd owns and operates a small business in Grafton, New South Wales. Doris employs part time staff to help her through busy periods. Her budgets for the next financial year show:

	$
Credit sales	140 000
Proceeds from sale of investments	8 400
Mortgage to be taken out at beginning of the year	9 800
Interest received on investments	700
Cash drawings	36 000
Receipts from accounts receivable	133 000
Casual wages	14 700
New capital introduced	49 000
Purchase of new plant	25 900
Cash sales	10 500
Operating expenses paid	31 500
Payments for goods	74 900
Depreciation expense	21 000
Repayment of short term loan	3 500
Dividends received on investments in shares	2 800
Cost of goods sold	91 000
Interest expense paid	4 900
Accrued wages	700
Cash balance — 1 July	28 000
Cash balance — 30 June	50 800

Required

Prepare a budgeted statement of cash flows for the coming financial year.

5.11 The cash budget for Saon Enterprises appears below.

Saon Enterprises

Cash budget for the year ending 30 June

	$	$
Cash balance 1 July — surplus		50 070
Receipts		
Cash sales	552 000	
Collections from accounts receivable	24 600	
Commission received	13 200	
Sale of motor vehicle	27 000	
Disposal of equipment	7 200	
Proceeds from loan	151 200	
Interest received from investments	13 800	
Sale of investments	96 000	885 000
Cash available for needs		935 070
Payments		
Salaries and wages	309 750	
Rates	5 580	
Telephone	1 740	
Bank and credit card fees	5 220	
Insurance	11 530	
Cash purchases	75 660	
Accounts payable	288 300	
Purchase of motor vehicles	39 150	
Acquisition of equipment	75 600	
Repayment of loan	22 680	
Drawings	24 780	
Purchase of investments	77 760	937 750
Cash balance 30 June — deficit		(2 680)

Required

Prepare a budgeted statement of cash flows for the coming financial year.

5.12 Carnabon Industries provides you with the following cash budget and other information:

Carnabon Industries

Cash budget for the month ending 30 November

	$	$
Beginning cash balance		27 000
Receipts		106 200
Cash sales	22 200	
Accounts receivable	84 000	
Cash available for needs		133 200
Payments		156 750
Purchases	66 750	
Selling and administration expenses	27 000	
Purchase of equipment	54 000	
Drawings	9 000	
Minimum cash balance		15 000
Total cash needed		171 750
Cash deficiency		38 550
Financing		38 550
Closing cash balance		15 000

- financing is by way of a short term bank loan
- $10 000 for wages is included in the selling and administration expenses.

Required
Prepare a budgeted statement of cash flows for November.

5.13 Aphrodite's Bounty specialises in bridal gowns and wedding accessories. Information relating to the budget period ending 30 September follows and the Trial balance as at 30 June is on page 116:

Sales	$
June (actual)	90 000
July	105 000
August	127 500
September	135 000
October	75 000

Aphrodite's Bounty

Trial balance as at 30 June

	$	$
Bank	13 500	
Accounts receivable	72 000	
Inventory	18 900	
Plant and equipment (net)	300 000	
Accounts payable		27 450
Capital		376 950
	404 400	404 400

- Twenty per cent of sales are for cash, the remainder are on credit. Credit sales are collected in the month following the sale.
- *Inventory and purchases:* Management requires a minimum closing inventory of 30% of the next month's cost of sales. Gross profit is 40% of sales. Purchases are 50% for cash and 50% on credit. Credit purchases are paid for in the month following purchase.
- *Expenses:* Expenses are paid in the month they are incurred. Marketing — fixed is $9000 per month; variable is 6% of sales. Administration — $14 250 per month, all fixed. This includes $3000 per month for depreciation. Financial — 4% of sales. This does not include any interest on borrowings to maintain minimum cash balance.
- *Other payments:* It is planned to purchase additional equipment, $29 625, in July. The proprietor will take drawings of $6000 in September.
- *Financing:* A minimum cash balance of $12 000 is required. Borrowing occurs at the beginning of the month when cash is needed. The exact amount required can be borrowed. Repayments (if appropriate) occur at the end of a month when cash is available. Interest is also paid in cash at the end of the month at an annual rate of 12% on the principal amount outstanding during the previous month. Explanation — if money is to be borrowed in July it is assumed it is borrowed on 1 July. Interest for July is paid at the end of August. Interest for August is paid at the end of September, and so on.
- Wages, salaries and commissions etc paid to employees are: July — $13 150; August — $13 825; September — $14 050. These are included in marketing, administration and financial expenses.

Required

Prepare the following:

(a) the sales budget for the three months ending 30 September, showing details of cash sales and credit sales

(b) the purchases budget for the three months ending 30 September

(c) the operating expenses budget for the three months ending 30 September
(d) the cash budget for the three months ending 30 September
(e) the budgeted revenue statement in summary format, showing monthly details, for the three months ending 30 September
(f) the budgeted balance sheet as at 30 September
(g) the budgeted statement of cash flows, showing monthly details, for the three months ending 30 September.

5.14 Gilgamesh Company had the following assets, liability, and capital at 30 September.

	$	$
Assets		
Bank		17 600
Accounts receivable (all collectable)		60 800
Inventory		105 600
Fixed assets	1 240 000	
less Accumulated depreciation	544 000	696 000
		880 000
Liability and capital		
Accounts payable		129 600
Capital		750 400
		880 000

- Budgeted sales are: October — $176 000; November — $160 000. All are on credit.
- Collections are expected to be 60% in the month of sale and 38% in the month following sale. The remainder are considered uncollectable. For budgeting purposes, bad debts are recognised in the month of sale.
- Sales are 125% of cost.
- In any given month, purchases represent 20% of the sales for that month and 80% of the sales for the following month.
- Purchases are paid for in the month following purchase.
- Operating expenses, to be paid in cash, are $18 000 per month.
- Annual depreciation is $172 800.

Required

Prepare the following:

(a) the cash budget for the month of October
(b) the budgeted revenue statement for October, in summary format
(c) the budgeted balance sheet as at 31 October.

5.15 Marduk Merchandisers have the following assets, liability and capital at 30 April.

	$
Assets	
Bank	50 000
Accounts receivable	45 000
Inventory	50 000
Plant and equipment (net)	140 000
	285 000
Liability and capital	
Accounts payable	40 000
Capital	245 000
	285 000

- May sales are budgeted at $100 000.
- Sales are 10% for cash and 90% on credit.
- Collections from accounts receivable are 60% in the month of sale and 40% in the month following sale.
- May purchases should be $30 000. All on credit.
- Accounts payable are paid 40% in the month of purchase and 60% in the month following purchase.
- Estimated inventory on 31 May is $30 000.
- Operating expenses to be paid in May are estimated at $40 000.
- Depreciation is budgeted at $10 000 for May.

Required

Prepare the following:

(a) the cash budget for May
(b) the budgeted revenue statement, in summary format, for May
(c) the budgeted balance sheet as at 31 May.

5.16 Handy Hardware is a retail hardware store. Information about the store's operations is given below.

- November sales amounted to $200 000.
- Sales are budgeted at $220 000 for December and $200 000 for January.
- Collections are expected to be 60% in the month of sale and 38% in the month following the sale. Two per cent of sales are expected to be uncollectable. Bad debts expense is recognised monthly.
- The store's gross margin is 25% of its sales revenue.
- A total of 80% of the merchandise for resale is purchased in the month prior to the month of sale, and 20% is purchased in the month of sale. Payment for merchandise is made in the month following the purchase.

- Other monthly expenses paid in cash amount to $22 600.
- Annual depreciation is $216 000.

The business's balance sheet as at 30 November is shown below:

Handy Hardware

Balance sheet as at 30 November

	$	$
Proprietor's funds		
Capital		938 000
Represented by:		
Current assets		238 000
Bank	22 000	
Accounts receivable (all collectible)	76 000	
Inventory	140 000	
Current liability		162 000
Accounts payable	162 000	
Working capital		76 000
Non-current assets		862 000
Property, plant and equipment	1 452 000	
less Accumulated depreciation	590 000	
Net assets		938 000

Required

Compute the following amounts:

(a) the budgeted cash collections for December
(b) the budgeted income (loss) for December
(c) the projected balance in accounts payable on 31 December.[2]

5.17 Thoth Enterprises had the following assets on 1 April:

	$	$
Bank		25 000
Accounts receivable (all March sales)		200 000
Inventory		37 500
Non-current assets	150 000	
less Accumulated depreciation	30 000	120 000

- There were no external liabilities.
- Budgeted sales are: April — $300 000; May — $287 500; June — $312 500.

- Eighty per cent of sales are on credit. Of these, 75% are collected in the first month after sale and the remainder in the second month after sale.
- Purchases are all on credit and amount to 60% of each month's sales value.
- Purchases are paid for 80% in the month of purchase, with a 5% discount, and the balance in the month after purchase.
- Operating expenses to be paid in cash each month are: marketing — $50 000; administration — $25 000; financial — $7500.
- Depreciation is 10% per annum using the straight line method. Depreciation is to be added to administration expenses.
- Estimated inventory at 30 June is $45 000.

Required

Prepare the following:

(a) the cash budget for the three months ending 30 June
(b) the budgeted revenue statement for the quarter ending 30 June — monthly details are not required
(c) the budgeted balance sheet as at 30 June.

Endnotes

1 Adapted from Langfield-Smith, K., Thorne, H. and Hilton, R., *Management Accounting: An Australian Perspective*, Sydney: NSW: McGraw-Hill Book Company, 1995
2 Langfield-Smith, Thorne, and Hilton

Chapter 6

Master budgets for manufacturing organisations

Objectives

By the end of this chapter you will be able to:

Introduction

Before considering budgets for manufacturing organisations it is beneficial to spend some time on a basic familiarisation of relevant concepts.

Berrivale Orchards Ltd in Berri, South Australia, has been manufacturing an extensive range of beverages and foods for more than fifty years. Ringgrip Pty Ltd of Dandenong, Victoria, makes electrical fittings and equipment. Zeitsch Bros, Grafton, New South Wales, produces carbonated soft drinks. These are just some examples of manufacturing organisations.

Manufacturing organisations are those businesses which produce goods.

You should now be able to do Question 6.1

Cost classifications

Product costs

Product costs are the costs of converting raw materials into a tangible finished item, for example, a television, stove or washing machine. These costs are allocated to the product and carried in inventories until the product is sold. Product costs can be categorised as:

- **raw materials** — required to make the product, for example, wood is used by Jindalee Craftworks to manufacture doors, cupboards, etc
- **direct labour** — the wages due to staff for the time spent in actually producing the goods
- **factory overhead** — all the other costs of running the factory, including depreciation of factory plant, rent or rates for factory premises, factory insurances and light and power used by the factory.

Also included in factory overhead are:

- *indirect materials*, which are small items of material used to produce goods, for example, nails, screws, glue, but their low cost does not justify keeping detailed records to trace them directly to the product — this group also includes factory supplies such as lubricating oils and cleaning rags
- *indirect labour*, which includes idle time, waiting time and other non-productive time of production staff; and wages for supervisors, cleaners and other staff not directly producing goods.

Period costs

Readers should already be familiar with period costs from previous studies. They are usually categorised as:
- **marketing, or selling and distribution expenses** — all the costs of marketing, selling and distributing the firm's products, for example, advertising, cartage outward and commission for sales people

- **general and administration expenses** — the costs incurred for the overall administration of the organisation, for example, general office salaries, audit fees, depreciation of computers for the accounting department
- **financial expenses** — those incurred in relation to financial aspects of the business, for example, interest paid on borrowings and discount allowed to debtors.

Self-test problem 6.1

Identify which of the following costs would be considered as period costs and which as product costs:

(a) metal used in the manufacture of motor vehicles
(b) advertising expense
(c) depreciation of desktop computers
(d) cartage of finished products to customers
(e) factory insurance
(f) oil used in a factory boiler
(g) bank charges
(h) cost of electricity for the general office
(i) production supervisor's salary
(j) rates on factory premises.

You should now be able to do Question 6.2

Direct costs

Direct costs are major items of cost that can be directly and relatively easily traced to the product.

Raw materials and direct labour are the items referred to here.

Indirect costs

Indirect costs are costs which cannot easily be traced directly to the product.

All factory overhead, including indirect materials and indirect labour, are indirect costs.

Self-test problem 6.2

Identify each of the following costs as direct or indirect:

(a) rags used for cleaning production equipment
(b) flour used to make bread
(c) depreciation of production machinery

(d) rates on factory
(e) wood and metal used to make desks
(f) oil used in a factory boiler
(g) oil used to lubricate production machinery
(h) meat used to make salami
(i) wages paid to employees while operating production machinery
(j) wages paid to supervisor of employees operating production machinery.

You should now be able to do Question 6.3

Inventories

Manufacturing organisations will usually have stocks of the following items on hand at any point in time.

Finished goods

These are fully completed products ready for sale.

Work in progress

These are partly completed goods that will be completed in the future. For example, at a particular point in time, a manufacturer of desks may have one batch of desks which are only partly assembled. At the same point in time there may be another batch of desks which are fully constructed but still need to be painted. The treatment of work in progress is more appropriate to cost and management accounting texts and is not a topic for this book.

Materials

Stocks of raw materials and factory supplies, for example, lubricants for machinery, are usually kept to ensure production is not held up due to lack of materials.

The manufacturing process

As indicated earlier the three main elements of cost for manufactured goods are direct materials, direct labour and factory overhead. Direct materials are input to production, these materials are processed and converted into products when direct labour and factory overhead are incurred. The output emerges in the form of finished goods ready for sale. Figure 6.1 illustrates the manufacturing process.

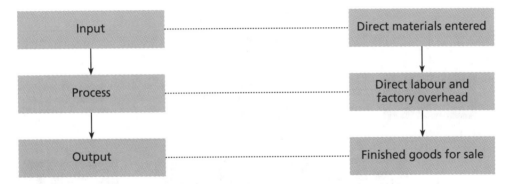

Figure 6.1 *The manufacturing process*[1]

You should now be able to do Question 6.4

Master budgets

Cairbre Containers manufactures cardboard boxes used for transporting wines, soft drinks, canned goods and the like. The company is preparing its master budget for the coming year ending 30 June. Figure 6.2 on page 126 shows the suite of budgets which make up the master budget for Cairbre Containers. Cairbre Containers will be used to illustrate the preparation of those budgets highlighted with shading in Figure 6.2. (The final two budgets are discussed on page 137.)

Data for Cairbre Containers

Sales

Cairbre Containers estimates that it will sell 900 000 boxes at $0.80 each during the coming year.

Direct materials

Each box requires an average of 0.4 kilograms of cardboard at a cost of $0.60 per kilogram.

Direct labour

It takes one hour to produce 300 boxes. Factory workers are paid an average of $15 per hour.

Factory overhead

The following factory overhead items are anticipated for the year:

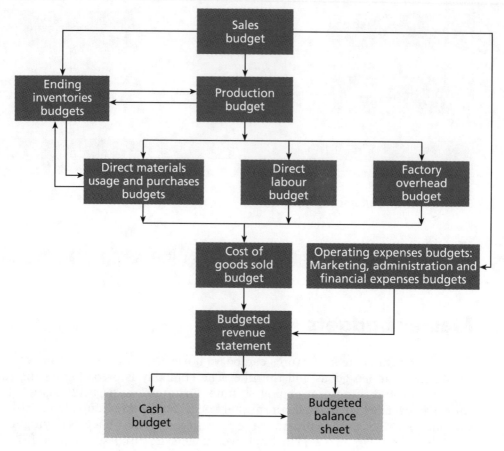

Figure 6.2 *Master budget for Cairbre Containers*

	$
Indirect materials	8 150
Indirect labour	43 500
Light and power	29 000
Rates	14 500
Factory insurances	17 500
Depreciation of factory equipment	21 000

Factory overhead is applied on the basis of direct labour hours. Application of factory overhead to production will be explained when the factory overhead budget is illustrated.

Inventories

Finished goods

Actual beginning inventory	29 000 boxes valued at $15 950
Desired ending inventory 30 June	20 000 boxes

Direct materials

Actual beginning inventory	6500 kg
Desired ending inventory 30 June	5000 kg

Operating expenses

Estimates for the year are:

Marketing

Advertising	2% of sales
Salespersons' salaries	$58 000

Administration

Management salaries and clerical wages	$110 000
Stationery, telephone, postage, etc	$14 500
Depreciation of office equipment	$9500

Financial

Bad debts	1% of sales
Bank charges etc	$5000

Tag the above information for easy reference

Sales budgets

The sales budget is prepared in the same fashion as demonstrated in Chapter 2.

Cairbre Containers

Sales budget for the year ending 30 June

	$
900 000 boxes at $0.80 per box	720 000

Production budgets

Recall the procedure used in Chapter 3 to prepare the purchases budget. The same procedure is used to compile the production budget.

Cairbre Containers

Production budget for the year ending 30 June

	Boxes
Sales	900 000
add Desired ending inventory	20 000
Total boxes needed	920 000
less Beginning inventory	29 000
Boxes to be produced	891 000

Self-test problem 6.3

Loreston Timeworks produces inexpensive kitchen clocks. Loreston had 400 clocks on hand at 1 January. Estimated sales for the three months ending 31 March are 6000 clocks. Ending inventory at 31 March is expected to be 550 clocks.

Required
Prepare the production budget for the quarter ending 31 March.

You should now be able to do Questions 6.5 and 6.6

Direct materials usage budgets

The purpose of the direct materials usage budget is to show the volume of direct materials which will be used in budgeted production. It can also show the value of the materials used.

Cairbre Containers

Direct materials usage budget for the year ending 30 June

Boxes to be produced (from production budget)	891 000
kg per box	× 0.4
Cardboard needed for production (kg)	356 400
Cost per kg	× $0.60
Cost of cardboard to be used in production	$213 840

Self-test problem 6.4

For the quarter ending 30 September, Storf Industries estimates its unit sales will be:

	Units
July	2 450
August	2 220
September	2 485

Desired inventories of finished goods are:

	Units
1 July	2 230
31 July	2 030
31 August	1 990
30 September	2 250

It takes four kilograms of raw materials to make each unit of product. Raw materials cost $3.60 per kilogram.

Required
Prepare a direct materials usage budget, showing volume and value, for the three months ending 30 September.

You should now be able to do Questions 6.7 and 6.8

Direct materials purchases budgets

The method used to prepare the direct materials purchases budget is:

- start with direct materials needed for production
- *add* the desired ending inventory of direct materials to find total direct materials needed
- *deduct* beginning inventory for direct materials to establish the quantity of direct materials to be purchased
- *multiply* the quantity to be purchased by the cost per purchase unit (in Cairbre Containers' case this is $0.60 per kilogram of cardboard).

Cairbre Containers

Direct materials purchases budget for the year ending 30 June	
Cardboard needed for production (kg)	356 400
add Desired ending inventory	5 000
Total cardboard needed	361 400
less Beginning inventory	6 500
Cardboard to be purchased (kg)	354 900
Price per kg	× $0.60
Cost of cardboard to be purchased	$212 940

Self-test problem 6.5

Estimated production in units for Dagda Company are: January — 7400; February — 8900; March — 8300; April — 8000. Three units of direct materials are required for each unit of finished product. Closing direct materials stock on hand is expected to be 60% of the following month's production expressed in terms of direct materials units. Direct materials cost $4 per unit.

Required
Prepare the direct materials purchases budget for the three months ending 31 March.

You should now be able to do Questions 6.9 to 6.12

Direct labour budgets

To prepare a direct labour budget it is necessary to establish the number of direct labour hours required to manufacture the budgeted production output and the labour cost for those hours.

In the Cairbre example the budgeted production output is the number of cardboard boxes to be produced. This is multiplied by the time taken to produce each box to give the total number of direct labour hours required for the production. The result is then multiplied by the labour cost per hour.

Cairbre Containers

Direct labour budget for the year ending 30 June	
Boxes to be produced	891 000
Boxes produced per hour	÷ 300
Direct labour required for production (hours)	2 970
Direct labour cost per hour	× $15
Total direct labour cost	$44 550

Self-test problem 6.6

Samsara Productions uses five direct labour hours to manufacture one unit of finished product. Direct labour costs $17.35 per hour. Samsara produces 1900 units per week and operates for 48 weeks of the year.

Required
Prepare the direct labour budget for the year ending 30 June.

You should now be able to do Questions 6.13 to 6.16

Factory overhead budgets

Each item of factory overhead must be estimated for the budget period. Cairbre Containers' factory overhead budget has been prepared from the original data.

Cairbre Containers

Factory overhead budget for the year ending 30 June

	$
Indirect materials	8 150
Indirect labour	43 500
Light and power	29 000
Rates	14 500
Factory insurances	17 500
Depreciation of factory equipment	21 000
Total factory overhead	133 650

Self-test problem 6.7

Renpet Industries provides you with the following information relating to factory overhead costs.

Expense item	Actual: Year 1 $	Expected increase: Year 2 %
Indirect labour	96 300	10
Indirect materials	39 100	15
Cleaning	35 500	5
Light and power	43 100	8
Rent	60 000	2
Insurance	34 400	6
Repairs and maintenance	39 900	5
Depreciation	30 000	5
Miscellaneous	28 600	12
	406 900	

Required
Prepare the factory overhead budget for the year ending 30 June, Year 2.

You should now be able to do Question 6.17

Factory overhead application rate

Because different items of overhead are incurred at different times of the year and it is difficult to trace overhead directly to a product, it is usual to charge the product with an estimated amount that is expected to cover the actual cost. This is done by establishing an application rate.

The application rate can be calculated on one of several bases, for example:

- per unit
- direct labour cost, or
- machine hours.

Cairbre's application rate is based on direct labour hours and is calculated by dividing budgeted factory overhead by the direct labour hours required for production:

$$\frac{\text{Budgeted factory overhead}}{\text{Budgeted direct labour hours required for production}} = \frac{\$133\,650}{2970}$$

$$= \$45 \text{ per direct labour hour}$$

Application of factory overhead

If Cairbre actually uses 250 direct labour hours in May of next year, production will be charged with 250 × $45 = $11 250 for factory overhead. That is, $11 250 will be applied to the product.

Self-test problem 6.8

Refer to Self-test problem 6.7. Budgeted direct labour hours are 9500 for Year 2.

Required
(a) What is Renpet Industries' application rate?
(b) If Renpet Industries uses 780 hours in February Year 2, how much factory overhead is applied to the product in February?

Self-test problem 6.9

You are provided with the following information for A. Business:

- estimated production for August is 7500 units
- fixed factory overhead for August is $12 000
- variable factory overhead rate is $1.75 per unit.

Required
Prepare the factory overhead budget for the month of August.

You should now be able to do Questions 6.18 and 6.19

Ending inventory budgets

Before the cost of goods sold budget and budgeted balance sheet can be prepared it is necessary to ascertain what the expected ending inventories will be. This is the function of the ending inventories budget.

Recall from earlier in this chapter that there are three basic types of inventories — finished goods, materials and work in progress. As work in progress is beyond the scope of this text only finished goods and direct materials will be illustrated.

To enable the calculation of finished goods inventory it is necessary to establish the cost of production for each completed unit:

- each box produced requires 0.4 kilograms of cardboard at $0.60 per kilogram
- each hour of direct labour produces 300 boxes at a cost of $15 for direct labour and $45 for factory overhead.

Therefore, the cost for each cardboard box is:

		$
Direct materials	(0.4 kg @ $0.60)	0.24
Direct labour	($15/300)	0.05
Factory overhead	($45/300)	0.15
		0.44

As the cost per kilogram of material is known, the ending inventory budget can be prepared.

Cairbre Containers

Ending inventory budget as at 30 June

		$
Finished goods	(20 000 boxes @ $0.44 per box)	8 800
Direct materials	(5000 kg @ $0.60 per kg)	3 000
Total ending inventories		11 800

Self-test problem 6.10

Each unit of finished product manufactured by Endorfin Concentrates requires:

- 2 litres of direct materials at a cost of $7 per litre
- 30 minutes of direct labour at $18 per hour.

Also note:

- factory overhead is applied at the rate of $20 per direct labour hour
- inventories at 30 November are estimated to be 3000 units of finished product and 5000 litres of direct materials.

Required
Prepare the ending inventories budget at 30 November.

You should now be able to do Question 6.20

Cost of goods sold budgets

The preparation of the cost of goods sold budget is similar to that of a retailer or wholesaler. The major difference is that the cost of production of finished goods is included instead of, or in addition to, purchases of finished goods.

All the information needed to compile the cost of goods sold budget is available from the original data or the budgets already prepared.

To calculate the cost of production, figures are taken from the direct materials usage budget, direct labour budget and factory overhead budget (or the factory overhead application rate is used). Cost of production is:

	$
Direct materials	213 840
Direct labour	44 550
Factory overhead	133 650
	392 040

The cost of goods sold budget will now be prepared.

Cairbre Containers

Cost of goods sold budget for the year ending 30 June

	$
Beginning finished goods inventory	15 950
Cost of production	392 040
Goods available for sale	407 990
less Ending finished goods inventory	8 800
Cost of goods sold	399 190

Self-test problem 6.11

The following details relate to Fravak Engineering.

- Fravak Engineering's production costs per unit are:

	$
Direct materials	22
Direct labour	30
Factory overhead	15

- Production is expected to be 5000 units in May.
- Inventories of finished product are estimated at:

	$
1 May	35 000
31 May	40 200

Required
Prepare the cost of goods sold budget for May.

You should now be able to do Question 6.21

Operating expenses budgets

The method used to prepare the marketing expenses budget, administration expenses budget and financial expenses budget is exactly the same as that described for service industries in Chapter 3.

The operating expenses budgets for Cairbre Containers appear below.

Cairbre Containers

Marketing expenses budget for the year ending 30 June

		$
Advertising	(2% × $720 000)	14 400
Salespersons' salaries		58 000
Total marketing expenses		72 400

Administration expenses budget for the year ending 30 June

	$
Management salaries and clerical wages	110 000
Stationery, telephone, postage, etc	14 500
Depreciation of office equipment	9 500
Total administration expenses	134 000

Financial expenses budget for the year ending 30 June

		$
Bad debts	(1% × $720 000)	7 200
Bank charges etc		5 000
Total financial expenses		12 200

You should now be able to do Question 6.22

Budgeted revenue statements

The technique used to prepare budgeted revenue statements as disclosed for service organisations in Chapters 3 and 5 is also appropriate for manufacturing organisations.

The budgeted revenue statement for Cairbre Containers follows.

Cairbre Containers

Budgeted revenue statement for the year ending 30 June

	$	$
Sales		720 000
less **Cost of goods sold**		399 190
Gross profit		320 810
less **Operating expenses**		218 600
Marketing	72 400	
Administration	134 000	
Financial	12 200	
Net profit		102 210

Self-test problem 6.12

Yasna and Zorya is a manufacturing organisation. It is in the process of producing its master budget. Budgets prepared to date are summarised below:

- from the sales budget:

		$
April	(3000 units @ $75 per unit)	225 000
May	(3600 units @ $80 per unit)	288 000
June	(3900 units @ $80 per unit)	312 000

- from the production budget:

	April	May	June
Sales — units	3 000	3 600	3 900
add Ending inventory	150	210	270
Units needed	3 150	3 810	4 170
less Beginning inventory	120	150	210
Units to be produced	3 030	3 660	3 960

- from the operating expenses budgets:

	April $	May $	June $
Marketing expenses	14 400	16 200	17 400
Administration expenses	18 000	20 250	21 750
Financial expenses	3 600	4 050	4 350

- Production for April and finished goods inventory on 1 April and 30 April costs $45 per unit.
- Production for May and June and finished goods inventory at 31 May and 30 June costs $50 per unit.

Required

Prepare the budgeted revenue statement, showing monthly details, for the three months ending 30 June.

You should now be able to do Question 6.23

Cash budget and budgeted financial statements

Manufacturing organisations prepare their cash budgets and budgeted financial statements using the same procedures that were demonstrated for service organisations in Chapters 4 and 5.

Varuna Manufacturing, which produces and sells souvenir cricket bats, will be used to illustrate the cash budget and budgeted financial statements for a manufacturing organisation.

Data for Varuna Manufacturing

Varuna's balance sheet at the end of the last financial year was:

Varuna Manufacturing

Balance sheet as at 30 June		
	$	$
Proprietor's funds		
Capital		309 600
Total proprietor's funds		309 600
Represented by:		
Current assets		230 500
Bank	60 000	
Accounts receivable	108 000	
Inventory — finished goods	52 500	
Inventory — direct materials	10 000	
Current liability		45 900
Accounts payable	33 900	
Loan from Bennu Finance Co.	12 000	
Working capital		184 600
Non-current assets		225 000
Plant and equipment	300 000	
less Accumulated depreciation	75 000	
		409 600
less **Non-current liability**		100 000
Loan from Bennu Finance Co.	100 000	
Net assets		309 600

Sales

Sales are anticipated to be $325 000 in July — 20% should be for cash and 80% on account.

Accounts receivable

Historically, collections from accounts receivable have been 55% in the month of sale and 45% in the month following sale. This pattern is expected to continue.

Inventories

Target ending inventories for 31 July are:

	$
Finished goods	60 000
Direct materials	10 000

Costs of production

Direct materials purchases are budgeted at $73 000. All purchases are on credit and are paid 65% in the month of purchase and 35% in the next month after purchase.

Direct labour and factory overhead are paid in the month incurred and are expected to be $60 000 and $40 000 respectively.

Operating expenses

To be paid in July, operating expenses are:

- marketing expenses — 15% of sales
- administration expenses — $53 000
- financial expenses — 5% of sales.

Depreciation

Depreciation is $3750 per month. This is to be included with administration expenses.

Loan repayment

This loan is repayable at $1000 per month — $1000 is to be repaid in July.

Budgets for Varuna Manufacturing

The cash budget and budgeted financial statements for Varuna Manufacturing, with supporting schedules and workings, are reproduced below.

- Sales:

		$
Cash	(20% × $325 000)	65 000
Credit	(80% × $325 000)	260 000
		325 000

- Collections from accounts receivable:

		$
From balance sheet		108 000
From July sales	(55% × $260 000)	143 000
		251 000

- Accounts receivable balance as at 31 July — 45% × $260 000 = $117 000.
- Payments to accounts payable:

		$
From balance sheet		33 900
From July purchases	(65% × $73 000)	47 450
		81 350

- Accounts payable balance as at 31 July — 35% × $73 000 = $25 550.
- Payment of operating expenses:

		$
Marketing	(15% × $325 000)	48 750
Administration (given)		53 000
Financial	(5% × $325 000)	16 250

- Loan from Bennu Finance Co. — non-current liability is $100 000 – $1000 = $99 000. As July for the year following the budget year becomes current for balance sheet purposes, it is the non-current portion of the loan which will be decreased in the balance sheet.

Varuna Manufacturing

Cash budget for the month ending 31 July

	$	$
Beginning balance — 1 July		60 000
Receipts		316 000
Cash sales	65 000	
Accounts receivable	251 000	
Cash available for needs		376 000
Payments		300 350
Accounts payable	81 350	
Direct labour	60 000	
Factory overhead	40 000	
Marketing expenses	48 750	
Administration expenses	53 000	
Financial expenses	16 250	
Loan from Bennu Finance Co.	1 000	
Closing balance — 31 July		75 650

Varuna Manufacturing

Budgeted revenue statement for the month ending 31 July

	$	$
Sales		325 000
less **Cost of goods sold**		165 500
Beginning inventory	52 500	
Cost of production	173 000	
Goods available for sale	225 500	
less Ending inventory	60 000	
Gross profit		159 500
less **Operating expenses**		121 750
Marketing	48 750	
Administration	56 750	
Financial	16 250	
Net profit		37 750

Varuna Manufacturing

Budgeted balance sheet as at 31 July

	$	$
Proprietor's funds		
Capital 1 July		309 600
add Net profit		37 750
Total proprietor's funds		347 350
Represented by:		
Current assets		262 650
Bank	75 650	
Accounts receivable	117 000	
Inventory — finished goods	60 000	
Inventory — direct materials	10 000	
Current liability		37 550
Accounts payable	25 550	
Loan from Bennu Finance Co.	12 000	
Working capital		225 100
Non-current assets		221 250
Plant and equipment	300 000	
less Accumulated depreciation	78 750	
		446 350
less **Non-current liability**		99 000
Loan from Bennu Finance Co.	99 000	
Net assets		347 350

You should now be able to do Questions 6.24 to 6.26

Checklist

Before progressing to the next chapter, complete the checklist below. This will identify whether you have an understanding of the important parts of the chapter.

Can you do the following?

❑ List some types of businesses operated by manufacturing organisations
❑ Give some examples of manufacturing organisations
❑ Define product costs, period costs, direct costs, indirect costs, direct materials, direct labour, factory overhead and inventories
❑ Explain the manufacturing process
❑ Compile sales budgets for manufacturing organisations
❑ Compile production budgets for manufacturing organisations
❑ Compile direct materials budgets for manufacturing organisations
❑ Compile direct labour budgets for manufacturing organisations
❑ Compile factory overhead budgets for manufacturing organisations
❑ Compile ending inventory budgets for manufacturing organisations
❑ Compile cost of goods sold budgets for manufacturing organisations
❑ Compile operating expense budgets for manufacturing organisations
❑ Compile cash budgets for manufacturing organisations
❑ Compile budgeted revenue statements for manufacturing organisations
❑ Compile budgeted balance sheets for manufacturing organisations

Questions

6.1   (a) Define a manufacturing organisation.
    (b) Name five organisations, other than those mentioned in this chapter, that carry on manufacturing activities.

6.2   For each of the following costs, identify whether they are product costs or period costs:

    (a) power for factory machinery
    (b) electricity for general office
    (c) chief accountant's salary
    (d) depreciation of factory machinery
    (e) salesperson's wages
    (f) repairs to factory machinery
    (g) insurance on factory buildings
    (h) motor vehicle expenses for sales manager's car
    (i) wages for lathe operator in a wood turning factory
    (j) wages for rest room attendant in a large factory.

6.3 For each of the following costs, indicate whether they would be considered direct or indirect:

(a) power for factory machinery
(b) wages paid to lathe operators for time spent turning piano legs
(c) wages paid to factory maintenance manager
(d) silicone used in glass manufacture
(e) fruit used to produce cordials
(f) repairs to factory machinery
(g) power for factory machinery
(h) screws and glue used in the manufacture of desks.

6.4 (a) Indicate and explain the typical inventories held by a manufacturing organisation.
(b) Briefly describe the manufacturing process.

6.5 McLennan Manufacturing expects that sales will be:

	Units
July	15 000
August	17 000
September	14 000
October	12 000

Management requires that beginning inventory of finished goods represent 40% of next month's sales.

Required

Prepare the production budget for the three months ending 30 September.

6.6 Oristo Company manufactures washing machines. Budgeted production for next month is 500 machines. Beginning inventory should be 50 machines and ending inventory is estimated at 67 machines.

Required

Calculate the budgeted sales for next month.

6.7 Saboc Manufacturing produces a 55 litre galvanised garbage bin. Relevant data for the period 1 October to 31 December includes:

• Sale price is $25 per garbage bin.
• Estimated number of bins to be sold:

	Bins
October	720
November	640
December	560
January	600

- *Direct materials:* Saboc uses 1.5 kilograms of galvanised metal in each bin. Galvanised metal costs $6 per kilogram. Management wants each month's beginning inventory to represent 25% of that month's production. Inventory at 31 December is 230 kilograms.
- *Direct labour:* Four garbage bins can be produced in one hour. Production personnel are paid an average of $15.50 per hour.
- *Factory overhead:* Fixed factory overhead is $400 per month. Variable factory overhead is $1 per bin. Factory overhead is applied at the rate of $1.625 per bin.
- *Finished goods inventory:* Management requires that each month's beginning inventory in units be 40% of that month's sales.

Required

Prepare the following:

(a) the sales budget for the three months ending 31 December
(b) the production budget for the three months ending 31 December
(c) the direct materials usage budget for the three months ending 31 December.

6.8 Caldwell Chemicals produces one product — XB14. For each litre of XB14 produced Caldwell inputs 0.3 litres of the material BRZ. Unit sales are estimated at:

	Litres
April	48 000
May	43 000
June	51 000
July	49 000

- Beginning inventory of XB14 is to be 25% of that month's sales.
- BRZ costs $50 per litre.

Required

Prepare the direct materials usage budget for the three months ending 30 June.

6.9 Kompira Ltd budgeted the following direct materials as necessary for production: July — 5890 units; August — 6960 units; September — 6670 units; October — 6570 units. Ending inventory of direct materials is required to be 50% of the following month's production expressed in terms of direct materials units. Cost of direct materials is $5 per unit.

Required

Prepare the direct materials purchases budget for the three months ending 30 September.

6.10 Refer to Question 6.7. Prepare the direct materials purchase budget for the three months ending 31 December.

6.11 Refer to Question 6.8. Closing inventory of BRZ is required to be 30% of the next month's production expressed in terms of litres of BRZ. Closing inventory of BRZ at 30 June is 4365 litres. Prepare the direct materials purchase budget for the three months ending 30 June.

6.12 Clear Pools Ltd, a manufacturer of swimming pool chemicals, plans to sell 200 000 units of finished product in July. Management anticipates a growth rate in sales of 5% per month. The desired monthly ending inventory of finished product is 80% of the next month's estimated sales. There are 150 000 finished units in the inventory on 30 June. Each unit of finished product requires 4 kilograms of direct materials at a cost of $1.20 per kilogram. There are 800 000 kilograms of direct materials in the inventory on 30 June.

Required

(a) Calculate Clear Pools' production requirements in units of finished product for the three month period ending 30 September.
(b) Independent of your answer to part (a), assume the company plans to produce 600 000 units of finished product in the three month period ending 30 September. The firm will have direct materials inventory at the end of the three month period equal to 25% of the direct materials used during that period. Calculate the estimated cost of direct materials purchases for the three month period ending 30 September.[2]

6.13 Heidrun Company manufactures tarpaulins. Each tarpaulin takes 30 minutes to produce. Average direct labour cost is $14 per hour. Estimated production of units for the coming quarter is: January — 1750; February — 3200; March — 4000.

Required

Prepare the direct labour budget for the three months ending 31 March.

6.14 Mimoro Crafts cuts, grinds, polishes and sets precious stones.

• The time taken to process each stone averages at:

	Mins
Cutting	15
Grinding	30
Polishing	20
Setting	45

- Direct labour costs per hour average:

	$
Cutting	12
Grinding	14
Polishing	15
Setting	20

- Estimated production for the month of May is 1200 finished items.

Required
Prepare the direct labour budget for the month of May.

6.15 PhotoArt Pty Ltd makes and sells artistic frames for photographs of special events. Bob Anderson, the company accountant, is responsible for preparing the company's annual budget. In compiling the budget data for the coming calendar year, Bob has learned that new automated production equipment will be installed on 1 March. This will reduce the direct labour per frame from 1 hour to 45 minutes. Labour-related costs include employer superannuation contribution of 6% of employee wages, workers' compensation insurance of $0.20 per hour, and payroll tax equal to 7% of employee wages. These 'on-costs' are treated as an additional direct labour cost. The accountant estimates that a wage increase for production workers of $2.00 per hour will take place on 1 April. Management expects to have 16 000 frames on hand at 1 January and has a policy of carrying an end of month inventory of 100% of the following month's sales plus 50% of the subsequent month's sales. This and other data compiled by Bob is summarised in the following table:

	January	February	March	April	May
Direct labour hours per unit	1.0	1.0	0.75	0.75	0.75
Wages per direct labour hour	$16.00	$16.00	$16.00	$18.00	$18.00
Estimated unit sales	10 000	12 000	8 000	9 000	9 000
Sales price per unit	$50.00	$47.50	$47.50	$47.50	$47.50

Required
Prepare a production budget and a direct labour budget for PhotoArt Pty Ltd, by month and for the first quarter of the budget year. Both budgets may be combined in one schedule. The direct labour budget should include direct labour hours and show the detail for each direct labour cost category.[3]

6.16 Refer to Question 6.7. Prepare the direct labour budget for the three months ending 31 December.

6.17 Brinkworth Corporation estimates that the factory overhead costs for the coming six months are:

	Jul. $	Aug. $	Sept. $	Oct. $	Nov. $	Dec. $
Depreciation	8 000	8 000	8 000	8 000	8 000	8 000
Supervisors' salaries	12 000	12 000	12 500	12 500	12 500	13 500
Indirect materials	8 000	7 500	8 100	7 900	8 200	6 500
Light and power	2 800	2 800	2 700	2 500	2 500	2 300
Repairs and maintenance	1 500	1 500	1 500	1 200	1 200	1 000
Insurance	600	600	600	600	600	600

Required

Prepare the factory overhead budget for the six months ending 31 December.

6.18 Refer to Question 6.7. Prepare the factory overhead budget for the three months ending 31 December.

6.19 Decan Fabrications has budgeted direct labour hours as follows: January — 6800; February — 7000; March — 8400. Budgeted factory overhead details are:

	$
Fixed (per month)	
Indirect materials	1 700
Indirect labour	2 100
Supervisor's wages	3 800
Repairs and maintenance	1 000
Light and power	1 250
Insurance	750
Rates	1 900
Depreciation	4 800
Variable (based on direct labour hours)	
Indirect labour	0.60
Payroll taxes	0.30
Repairs and maintenance	0.20
Light and power	0.40
Miscellaneous	0.20

Required

Prepare the factory overhead budget for the three months ending 31 March.

6.20 Refer to Question 6.7. Prepare the ending inventory budget at 31 December.

6.21 Tursas Productions' manufacturing costs per unit are:

	$
Direct materials	15
Direct labour	13
Factory overhead	22
	50

Production, in units, for the quarter ending 31 December is: October — 1960; November — 2090; December — 1740. Inventories of finished product are expected to be:

	Units
1 October	310
31 October	380
30 November	460
31 December	340

Required

Prepare the cost of goods sold budget for the three months ending 31 December.

6.22 Kumanu Company provides the following information:

- Projected sales of manufactured product for the quarter ending 31 March: January — $117 000; February — $120 000; March — $131 000.
- Salaries are fixed at $17 000 per month and are allocated: marketing — 40%; administration — 50%; financial — 10%.
- Variable expenses are budgeted as a percentage of sales: commissions — 3%; advertising — 2%; bad debts — 1%.
- Remaining expenses (all fixed) per month are: depreciation — $1120 allocated half to marketing and half to administration; insurance — $530 treated as administration; miscellaneous — $1100 allocated 30% to marketing, 70% to administration, and 10% to financial.

Required

Prepare the following for the three months ending 31 March:

(a) the marketing expenses budget

(b) the administration expenses budget
(c) the financial expenses budget.

6.23 Hurons Manufacturing produces a single product identified as PFR. Data relating to the coming month are:

- *Sales:* Estimated at 12 500 units. Selling price will be $95 per unit.
- *Inventories:* Beginning inventories — finished goods 750 units valued at $48 000; direct materials 2000 kilograms valued at $9500. Desired ending inventory — finished goods 1000 units; direct materials 2500 kilograms.
- *Cost per manufactured unit:* Direct materials — 3 kilograms at $5 per kilogram; direct labour — 2 hours at $15 per hour; factory overhead — 2 hours at $10.
- *Operating expenses:* Marketing expenses are 10% of sales; administration expenses are $87 500 per month; financial expenses are 5% of sales.

Required
Prepare the budgeted revenue statement for the coming month.

6.24 Regin and Ament produce wooden artefacts. Budgeted sales are: June — $210 000; July — $273 000; August — $231 000. Budgeted costs of production are:

	June $	July $	August $
Direct materials purchases	44 100	66 150	48 510
Direct labour paid	50 400	75 600	55 440
Factory overhead paid	31 500	47 250	34 650

- Collections from customers are 70% in the month of sale, 20% in the month following sale, and 9% in the second month following the sale — 1% are expected to be bad debts.
- Direct materials purchases are paid for in the month after purchase and receive a 2% discount.
- Cash payments for operating expenses are estimated at $50 400 for August.
- Regin and Ament's bank balance on 1 August is $77 000.

Required
Prepare the cash budget for the month of August.

6.25 Triton Metalcraft manufactures garden benches. Its trial balance at 30 June shows:

	$	$
Bank	22 685	
Accounts receivable	28 470	
Materials inventory	24 100	
Finished goods inventory	41 500	
Prepaid expenses	4 400	
Plant and equipment	341 000	
Accumulated depreciation — plant and equipment		68 300
Accounts payable		99 700
Mortgage		114 400
Capital		179 755
	462 155	462 155

Information extracted from budgets for the quarter ending 30 September showed:

	$
Material purchases	62 530
Material usage	65 300
Direct labour expenses	94 750
Factory overhead expenses	53 150
Marketing expenses	59 560
Administration expenses	78 300
Cost of goods manufactured	213 200
Cost of goods sold	215 100
Sales	536 850

- Accounts receivable should increase 200% during the quarter.
- Accounts payable will decrease by 30%.
- Mortgage payments for the quarter will be $7800, of which $2600 is interest expense.
- Prepaid expenses should rise by $26 000.
- Depreciation for plant and equipment (already included in the factory overhead budget) is 15% per annum.
- A motor vehicle will be purchased late in September at an estimated price of $27 000.

Required

(a) Prepare the budgeted revenue statement for the quarter ending 30 September.
(b) Prepare the budgeted balance sheet as at 30 September.

6.26 Olwen Company manufactures a single product. The master budget for February is about to be prepared. The following information is available.

- *Sales:* Estimated sales in units for February are 4900. Selling price will be $100 per unit.
- *Inventories:* Finished goods — 1 February 340 units valued at $19 550; desired at 28 February 520 units. Direct materials — 1 February, 210 kilograms valued at $2100; desired at 28 February, 180 kilograms.
- *Cost of production:* Direct materials — 2 kilograms of material is needed to produce each unit of finished goods at a cost of $10 per kilogram; direct labour — 1.5 hours of direct labour are required to complete each unit of finished goods and direct labour costs $18 per hour; factory overhead — variable factory overhead for February is expected to be $25 440 and fixed overhead $27 900 and the factory overhead is applied to production on the basis of machine hours where each finished unit requires 1 machine hour.

Required

Prepare, for the month of February:

(a) the sales budget
(b) the production budget
(c) the direct materials purchases budget
(d) the direct labour budget
(e) the factory overhead budget and calculate the factory overhead application rate
(f) the cost of goods sold budget.

Endnotes

1 Adapted from Neish, W. and Banks, A., *Management Accounting: Principles and Applications*, Sydney, NSW: McGraw-Hill Book Company, 1996
2 From Langfield-Smith, K., Thorne, H. and Hilton, R., *Management Accounting: An Australian Perspective*, Sydney, NSW: McGraw-Hill Book Company, 1995
3 From Langfield-Smith, Thorne, and Hilton

Chapter 7

Performance reports

Introduction

Recall that controlling is the process of setting standards; measuring current performance and comparing it against the standards; and, where necessary, taking remedial action. This is illustrated in Figure 1.1 on page 2.

Note that:

- plans, including budgets, are prepared
- action is taken to implement the plans
- performance is measured by comparing actual results to budget — differences, or variances, are analysed by management to see what action needs to be taken
- remedial action is adopted, if necessary, or plans are reviewed and reassessed.

It is normal for an organisation to compare actual results with budgets by preparing performance reports.

This chapter concentrates on performance reports based on static budgets. In Chapter 8 performance reports using flexible budgets based on actually achieved levels will be illustrated.

Organisation structure

Clarenza Industries is a diversified conglomerate. Its operations include building products, marine products, homewares and transport.

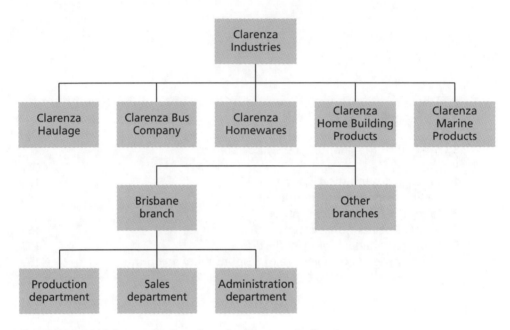

Figure 7.1 *Partial organisation chart for Clarenza Industries*

Figure 7.1 shows a simplified organisation chart for Clarenza Industries. An organisation chart depicts the structure of an organisation and shows the lines of responsibility and communication within that organisation.

Organisations are usually structured on one or more of the following bases.

Functional

The organisation is divided into sub-units which can be identified by the functions they perform. At the individual branch level for Clarenza Home Building Products departments have been created for the functions of production, sales and administration. Each department has its own supervisor who is responsible to the branch manager.

Geographic

The organisation's sub-units may be delineated by location. Clarenza Home Building Products has branches in Brisbane, Sydney, Melbourne, Adelaide and Perth. Each branch manager is responsible to the general manager, Clarenza Home Building Products.

Product

Many multi-product companies, such as BHP and CSR, are organised by product. In Clarenza's case each division represents a distinct product group. The divisional general managers report to the managing director of Clarenza Industries.

Self-test problem 7.1

Lanitza Holdings provides products for the rural community. Each product line is manufactured by a separate division. There are divisions for farm machinery, fertilisers, outdoor clothing and stock feed. Each division is organised by department. The departments for the farm machinery division are: materials and procurement; production; sales; personnel; and administration and accounts. These departments are then divided into smaller units. The materials and procurement department is separated into purchasing, receiving, storing and issuing.

Required

Prepare a partial organisation chart for Lanitza Holdings. Use Figure 7.1 as an example.

You should now be able to do Question 7.1

Responsibility accounting

Individual members of business units are responsible for various tasks and functions. When individuals work together to achieve organisational goals this is known as **goal congruence**.

A management accounting system which attempts to encourage goal congruence is called **responsibility accounting**.

Refer again to Figure 7.1. Note that the Brisbane branch manager is responsible for the performance of that branch and reports to the divisional general manager.

It is necessary to have some yard stick by which Brisbane's performance can be measured. This is usually achieved by setting budgets. Actual results can then be compared to budget.

Responsibility accounting is a system whereby actual results, for each sub-unit in an organisation, are measured against budget and significant variances investigated.

Responsibility centres

For responsibility accounting a division, branch, department or other sub-unit is known as a **responsibility centre**.

A responsibility centre is an organisational sub-unit whose manager is accountable for the activities and performance of the sub-unit. Responsibility centres can be identified as one of the following.

Cost centre

A **cost centre** is an organisational sub-unit, for example, department or section, where the manager is accountable for costs only. The production department at Brisbane branch of Clarenza Home Building Products is a cost centre.

Revenue centre

A **revenue centre** is an organisational sub-unit where the manager is accountable for revenue earned. The sales department at Brisbane is a revenue centre.

Profit centre

A **profit centre** is an organisational sub-unit, for example, division or branch, where the manager is accountable for profit and thus both revenues and costs. Brisbane branch is a profit centre as it would be expected to make a profit from its operations.

Investment centre

An **investment centre** is an organisational sub-unit, such as a division or the entire organisation, where the manager is held accountable for the profit and the capital invested in the centre. The building products division is an investment centre if the general manager has the authority to open new branches or institute expansion of existing branches.

The managing director of Clarenza Industries makes the final decision on whether or not to attempt a take over of a competitor or set up a new division. Clarenza Industries is an investment centre.

Self-test problem 7.2

For each of the following organisational sub-units indicate the type of responsibility centre:

(a) the sales department of a brewery
(b) an orange juice factory operated by a large orange grower
(c) the business studies department at a TAFE college
(d) the Australian subsidiary of an American multi-national company
(e) the mayor's office in a large city
(f) the reservations department of a national bus company
(g) a company-owned restaurant in a fast food chain
(h) the claims department in an insurance company.

You should now be able to do Question 7.2

Performance reports

Department managers at Clarenza Home Building Products' Brisbane branch are accountable for their departments and responsible to the branch manager. Each branch manager is accountable for the performance of the branch and responsible to the general manager, Clarenza Home Building Products. The divisional general managers are, in turn, accountable for their respective divisions and responsible to the managing director of Clarenza Industries.

In addition to normal verbal and written communication, **performance reports** are prepared on a regular basis, at least monthly. A performance report shows budget and actual figures and any variances which may arise. More detailed performance reports may provide for explanatory comments by the manager who is responsible.

Figure 7.2 on page 156 illustrates performance reports for various levels of Clarenza Industries.

A **variance** is the difference between budget and actual. *F* indicates a **favourable variance**. This means that actual income exceeds budgeted income or actual cost is less than budgeted cost. *U* indicates an **unfavourable variance**. An unfavourable variance is the outcome of actual income being less than budgeted income or actual cost exceeding budgeted cost.

Well designed performance reports provide detailed information allowing management to analyse performance and identify responsibility.

- The bottom section of the report in Figure 7.2 shows the results for the Brisbane cost centre, administration department.
- Working up the report, total costs for the administration department are then collated with the results of other departments to show the profit for the profit centre — Brisbane branch.
- The profits and losses of all branches and head office are combined to show the overall profit for the Home Building Products Division.
- The results for all divisions are coordinated into a summary final report for Clarenza Industries.

The reasons for variances are numerous. Here are a couple of examples from Brisbane branch to illustrate this.

- The administration department has a $1620 *U* (unfavourable variance) for salaries in April. It is possible that a staff member went on holidays towards the end of April which meant that their holiday pay was paid in April but may have been budgeted as normal pay for May. It is also possible that a new enterprise agreement was negotiated that gave office staff a pay rise which had not been included in the budget. These could also explain the year to date variance.

Clarenza Industries
Performance reports for April
for selected sub-units

	April			Year to date		
	Budget $	Actual $	Variance $	Budget $	Actual $	Variance $
To Clarenza Industries	742 020	715 686	26 334 U	5 996 400	6 065 250	68 850 F
Home Building Products division						
Head office	(95 150)	(110 500)	15 350 U	(1 046 460)	(1 017 160)	29 300 F
Adelaide	97 500	90 240	7 260 U	900 000	932 750	32 750 F
Brisbane	101 670	135 096	33 426 F	912 860	896 620	16 240 U
Melbourne	200 000	187 910	12 090 U	1 600 000	1 549 320	50 680 U
Sydney	240 000	220 000	20 000 U	1 980 000	1 950 000	30 000 U
Perth	198 000	192 940	5 060 U	1 650 000	1 753 720	103 720 F
	742 020	715 686	26 334 U	5 996 400	6 065 250	68 850 F
Brisbane branch						
Sales	506 120	674 820	168 700 F	4 394 500	4 146 400	248 100 U
Production	(379 590)	(513 320)	133 730 U	(3 232 740)	(2 998 320)	234 420 F
Administration	(24 860)	(26 404)	1 544 U	(248 900)	(251 460)	2 560 U
	101 670	135 096	33 426 F	912 860	896 620	16 240 U
Administration						
Salaries	21 000	22 620	1 620 U	210 000	212 400	2 400 U
Stationery	750	690	60 F	7 800	7 920	120 U
Telephone	840	864	24 U	9 000	9 240	240 U
Electricity	1 020	960	60 F	9 600	9 300	300 F
Rates	500	520	20 U	5 000	5 100	100 U
Depreciation	750	750	—	7 500	7 500	—
	24 860	26 404	1 544 U	248 900	251 460	2 560 U

Figure 7.2 *Clarenza Industries*

- Brisbane's overall performance for April looks good. It had a $33 426 *F* (favourable variance). This may be because a new housing development has commenced which was not anticipated in the budget.
- The branch's performance for the year to date is not so good and may be accounted for by the fact that the area was slower to recover from an economic recession than, say, Adelaide or Perth.

Self-test problem 7.3

The personnel department of Lanitza Holdings' Farm Machinery division had the following budget for the current year:

	$
Salaries	161 700
Stationery	3 626
Telephone	6 720
Electricity	7 834
Office rent	18 000
Depreciation	6 100
	203 980

Assume the budget for December for the personnel department was 9% of the year's total budget for salaries; 7.5% for stationery, telephone and electricity; and one twelfth for office rent and depreciation. Actual results for December were:

	$
Salaries	15 100
Stationery	256
Telephone	478
Electricity	569
Office rent	1 550
Depreciation	508
	18 461

Required
Prepare a performance report for December. Calculations may be made to the nearest dollar.

You should now be able to do Question 7.3

Management by exception

Managers cannot possibly keep track of every little detail concerned with operating a business. The principle of **management by exception** is often used to enable management to concentrate on problem situations or other matters that require attention.

Management by exception means that the appropriate person is notified when there is a significant deviation from plan. Performance reports can be used to highlight the areas needing attention by expressing each variance as a percentage of budget. Only those items that exceed an acceptable limit, for example plus or minus 5%, will be investigated.

Refer again to Figure 7.2. The April figures for Brisbane's administration department will be used to illustrate management by exception.

Clarenza Home Building Products Division

**Brisbane branch: Administration department
for the month of April**

	Budget $	Actual $	Variance $	Variance %
Salaries	21 000	22 620	1 620 *U*	7.71 *U*
Stationery	750	690	60 *F*	8.00 *F*
Telephone	840	864	24 *U*	2.86 *U*
Electricity	1 020	960	60 *F*	5.88 *F*
Rates	500	520	20 *U*	4.00 *U*
Depreciation	750	750	——	
	24 860	26 404	1 544 *U*	6.21 *U*

The formula for calculating the variance percentage is:

$$\frac{Variance}{Budget} \times 100$$

For salaries this is:

$$\frac{1\,620}{21\,000} \times 100 = 7.71\%$$

The total of the variance percentage column was calculated:

$$\frac{1\,544}{22\,860} \times 100 = 6.21\%$$

Note that this is not the sum of the figures in this column.

Clarenza's policy is to investigate all variances which deviate from budget by plus or minus 5%. Under this policy the variances for salaries, stationery and electricity will be investigated. Although the variances for stationery and electricity are favourable and the dollar amounts relatively small, it is still wise to investigate these, if for no other reason than that the budget may need to be adjusted.

Self-test problem 7.4

Refer to Self-test problem 7.3.

Required
(a) Recast the performance report to show the percentage deviation from budget for each variance.
(b) Lanitza Holdings' policy is to investigate all variances which deviate by plus or minus 5% from budget. Identify items to be investigated.

You should now be able to do Questions 7.4 and 7.5

Responsibility accounting and blame

Responsibility accounting is *not* concerned with trying to find who is to blame. Placing blame leads to defensive behaviour and game-playing by organisational members. Their major objective becomes ensuring that they achieve their set targets and budgets *at all costs*, regardless of the consequences to others in the organisation or the likely effect their behaviour will have on attaining organisational goals.

A properly used responsibility accounting system **provides information** and **identifies who should be consulted** about specific situations or variances.

You should now be able to do Questions 7.6 to 7.12

Checklist

Before progressing to the next chapter, complete the checklist below. This will identify whether you have an understanding of the important parts of the chapter.

Can you do the following?

☐ Prepare an organisation chart
☐ Define responsibility accounting
☐ Identify each type of responsibility centre
☐ Prepare performance reports
☐ Explain management by objectives
☐ Identify which variances need investigating
☐ Identify the major objective of responsibility accounting

Questions

7.1 Diamond Bay Corporation's operations consist of ten hotels and resorts. The organisation is divided into two divisions. The Queensland division operates four resorts at Cairns, Townsville, Mackay and Hervey Bay; and two hotels in Brisbane and Mermaid Beach. The New South Wales division has three hotels in Sydney, Newcastle and Wollongong; and a resort at Byron Bay. The Diamond Mask Hotel in Sydney is organised into the following departments: grounds and maintenance; house-keeping; recreational services; and food and beverages. The food and beverages department is further subdivided into banquets and catering; restaurants; and kitchen.

Required

Prepare a partial organisation chart for the Diamond Bay Corporation.

7.2 (a) Define responsibility accounting.
(b) What is a responsibility centre?
(c) Identify four types of responsibility centre and give an example of each, other than those used in this chapter.

7.3 The kitchen of the Diamond Mask Hotel had the following figures:

	Two months 1 Jul–31 Aug		Month of September	
	Budget $	Actual $	Budget $	Actual $
Kitchen staff wages	94 400	96 000	48 000	48 800
Food	795 200	798 400	386 400	384 800
Paper products	140 000	136 000	70 400	68 000
Cleaning materials etc	12 000	11 500	6 000	5 700
Electricity	36 000	36 800	18 000	18 200
Rent	20 000	20 000	10 000	10 000
Depreciation	25 000	25 800	12 500	12 900

Required

Prepare a performance report showing budget, actual and variances for the month of September and the year to 30 September.

7.4 Refer to Question 7.3.

(a) Using only the figures for the month of September, prepare a performance report that includes the percentage deviation from budget for each variance.

(b) Diamond Mask Hotel has a policy which requires all variances that deviate plus or minus 3% from budget to be investigated. Which variances should be investigated?

7.5 Explain management by exception.

7.6 Nielson Products make wooden toys. The toys are made in the assembly department. When fully constructed, the toys are put onto an endless chain of hooks which move continuously through the painting department and into a drying oven. Department managers are responsible for the costs and production of their respective departments. Failure of some spray painting equipment meant that the toys had to be removed from the hooks and returned later when the equipment was operational. As the assembly department controls the chain of hooks the painting manager requested the assembly manager to stop production until the spray painting equipment was repaired. The assembly manager's reaction was, 'Not likely. I've got my budget to meet, you know!' The labour and overhead costs incurred during the downtime in the painting department amounted to $7424. The manager of the painting department claims these costs should be charged to assembly because the painters would have repaired the equipment in less time if they hadn't spent their time removing toys from the hooks and storing them.

Required
How should the $7424 be dealt with? Justify your answer.

7.7 Caleb Constructions provides you with the following figures for its factory overhead for the month of August:

	Budget $	Actual $
Indirect materials	50 400	63 840
Indirect labour	96 000	96 480
Maintenance	21 600	6 480
Electricity	6 900	7 200
Insurance	6 480	6 440
Lease of building	11 200	11 500
Depreciation of plant	12 720	12 720

Required
(a) Prepare a performance report for August showing the percentages of variances from budget.
(b) Caleb's policy is to investigate all variances which deviate plus or minus 5% from budget. Which variances should be investigated?

7.8 Ms H. Crypt is the manager of the clothing department of a department store. Following is a summary of the department's figures for December:

	Budget $	Actual $
Sales		
Men's clothing	31 235	29 465
Women's clothing	56 230	65 475
Children's clothing	37 485	36 010
Total sales	124 950	130 950
Cost of goods sold		
Men's clothing	20 135	20 030
Women's clothing	36 250	44 505
Children's clothing	24 165	24 480
Sales commission	7 800	7 990
Sales salaries	3 000	3 150
Supervisors salaries	3 600	3 600
Advertising	12 150	12 975
Depreciation	3 300	3 825
Insurances	375	375
Financial expenses	450	505
Total expenses	111 225	121 435
Net profit	13 725	9 515

Required

Prepare a performance report, in revenue statement format, for the month of December.

7.9 The Boardwalk Copying Service had the following data for November:

	Budget $	Actual $
Paper products bought and used	2 560	2 790
Variable overhead	320	190
Fixed overhead	960	1 030
Revenue from copying services	3 520	3 230
Revenue from laminating	880	940

Required

(a) Prepare a performance report which shows the percentages for variances.
(b) If Boardwalk investigates those variances which deviate plus or minus 5% from budget, which variances should be investigated?

7.10 M. Maher is a solicitor. The overhead budget for the current financial year shows:

	$
Support labour	75 000
Stationery	6 000
Travel	15 000
Phones/faxes	1 500
Photocopying	300
Rent	11 700
Depreciation	4 500

- It is anticipated that $360 000 will be earned in legal fees and estimated cost of professional labour is $150 000.
- The total budget is apportioned equally each month.
- Actual results for the month of October and the four months ended 31 October were:

	October $	Year to date $
Fees income	27 000	122 000
Professional labour	12 000	50 400
Support labour	6 600	26 000
Stationery	450	1 800
Travel	900	4 000
Phone/faxes	135	520
Photocopying	20	90
Rent	975	3 900
Depreciation	375	1 500

Required
Prepare a performance report for the month of October and the four months ended 31 October.

7.11 The Hochimin is an oriental restaurant specialising in Thai and Vietnamese food. The following estimates were made for the financial year ended 30 June:

- Estimated sales: 30 000 at $25 each — 50% of sales are for cash and 50% are paid for by credit card. The restaurant receives 95% of the value of credit card sales.

- Estimated costs:

Ingredients for meals	$10 per meal
Direct labour	$5 per meal
Light and power	$2 per meal
Cleaning materials etc	$1 per meal
Depreciation	$10 000
Indirect labour	$30 000
Rent	$20 800
Motor vehicle expenses	$5000
Take away containers	$7000
Advertising	$8000

- Bank account balance at start of year — $30 000.
- New furniture will be purchased in February at an estimated cost of $40 000.
- Actual results for the year were:

	$
Sales	789 750
Ingredients for meals	330 000
Direct labour	170 000
Light and power	64 000
Cleaning materials etc	28 500
Depreciation	11 000
Indirect labour	29 000
Rent	22 000
Motor vehicle expenses	4 700
Take away containers	8 500
Advertising	7 500
New furniture	37 000

Required

Prepare a cash budget performance report for the year ended 30 June.

7.12 Clifford Enterprises had the following figures for the financial year ended 30 June:

	$
Budget	
Sales	156 375
Cost of goods sold	76 500
Marketing expenses	19 350
Administration expenses	15 525
Financial expenses	5 400

	$
Actual	
Sales	168 000
Cost of goods sold	83 250
Marketing expenses	23 000
Administration expenses	15 500
Financial expenses	4 250

Required

Prepare a revenue statement performance report to comply with the requirements of management by exception.

Chapter 8

Flexible budgets

Introduction

All the budgets illustrated so far have been static budgets. Recall from Chapter 1 that a **static budget** is prepared for a particular, planned level of activity. In contrast, a **flexible budget** covers a range of activity within which an organisation might operate.

Consider the performance report for Pandion Trophies Ltd shown on page 167.

It certainly seems that Pandion has had a bad year. The company fell 5000 units short of its sales target, but how can its performance in other areas be judged? For a more realistic comparison it is necessary to compare a budget prepared for 75 000 units with the actual figures. To do this it is first necessary to identify which expenses are fixed and which are variable. Remember that fixed costs remain the same amount, in total, within the relevant range of activity. Variable costs increase or decrease, in total, as activity increases or decreases.

Pandion Trophies Ltd

Performance report for the year ended 30 June

	Budget Units	Actual Units	Variance Units
Trophies sold	80 000	75 000	5 000 *U*
	$	$	$
Sales	500 000	450 000	50 000 *U*
less **Cost of goods sold**	387 500	365 000	22 500 *F*
Gross profit	112 500	85 000	27 500 *U*
less **Operating expenses**			
Selling	30 000	27 000	3 000 *F*
Administration	20 000	18 750	1 250 *F*
Financial	7 500	7 300	200 *F*
Total operating expenses	57 500	53 050	4 450 *F*
Net profit	55 000	31 950	23 050 *U*

Having identified fixed and variable costs the performance report could be recast as follows:

Pandion Trophies Ltd

Performance report for the year ended 30 June

	Budget Units	Actual Units	Variance Units
Trophies sold	80 000	75 000	5 000 *U*
	$	$	$
Sales	500 000	450 000	50 000 *U*
less **Variable costs**	370 000	340 000	30 000 *F*
Contribution margin	130 000	110 000	20 000 *U*
less **Fixed costs**	75 000	78 050	3 050 *U*
Net profit	55 000	31 950	23 050 *U*

The **contribution margin** is found by deducting all variable costs from sales. The contribution margin is the amount that is available to cover, or contribute to, fixed costs and profit.

Note that at this stage a comparison at the 75 000 unit level has not been made.

Self-test problem 8.1

Anshar Manufacturing makes ball point pens. Its budgeted revenue statement for the coming year shows:

Anshar Manufacturing

Budgeted revenue statement for the year ending 30 June

	$	$	$
Sales (200 000 pens)			400 000
less **Cost of goods sold**			260 000
Direct materials		140 000	
Direct labour		48 000	
Variable factory overhead		32 000	
Fixed factory overhead		40 000	
Gross profit			140 000
less **Operating expenses**			61 000
Selling		28 000	
Variable expenses	22 000		
Fixed expenses	6 000		
Administration and financial		33 000	
Variable expenses	8 000		
Fixed expenses	25 000		
Net profit			79 000

Required

Recast the budgeted revenue statement so that all variable costs are grouped together, all fixed costs are grouped together, and contribution margin is shown. *Remember:* Direct materials and direct labour are variable costs.

Flexible budget equation

Having identified budgeted fixed and variable costs it is possible to express the relationship between activity and total expenses as a formula:

$$\text{Total budgeted expenses} = \left[\left(\begin{array}{l} \text{Budgeted} \\ \text{variable costs} \\ \text{per activity unit} \end{array} \times \begin{array}{l} \text{Total} \\ \text{activity} \\ \text{units} \end{array} \right) + \begin{array}{l} \text{Budgeted} \\ \text{fixed} \\ \text{costs} \end{array} \right]$$

Pandion Trophies Ltd needs to calculate the budgeted variable costs per activity unit. Pandion's activity is measured in number of units sold, so:

$$\frac{\textit{Budgeted variable costs}}{\textit{Budgeted trophies sold}} = \frac{\$370\,000}{80\,000} = \$4.625 \text{ per trophy}$$

Pandion's flexible budget formula is:

Total budgeted expenses = [($4.625 × no. of trophies sold) + $75 000]

Note that in this example the activity was the number of units sold. It could easily have been sales dollars, machine hours or some other measure of activity. The average budgeted sales price for trophies is ($500 000/80 000) $6.25.

Self-test problem 8.2

Refer to Self-test problem 8.1.

Required
(a) What is the flexible budget equation?
(b) What is the average budgeted sale price for pens?

You should now be able to do Question 8.1

Preparation of flexible budgets

Before comparing Pandion's performance at the 75 000 unit activity level it is proposed to illustrate the preparation of flexible budgets.

Suppose Pandion Trophies Ltd anticipated that there was a probability that the actual activity level might differ from the master budget. Management would want to see the effect on profits of other likely activity levels. The following flexible budget could be prepared:

Pandion Trophies Ltd

Flexible budget for the year ending 30 June

	Units	Units	Units	Units
Trophies sold	70 000	75 000	80 000	85 000
	$	$	$	$
Sales	437 500	468 750	500 000	531 250
less **Variable expenses**	323 750	346 875	370 000	393 125
Contribution margin	113 750	121 875	130 000	138 125
less **Fixed expenses**	75 000	75 000	75 000	75 000
Net profit	38 750	46 875	55 000	63 125

Master budget

Using the activity level of 70 000 trophies to illustrate, calculations were made as follows:

- sales are ($6.25 × 70 000) $437 500
- variable costs are ($4.625 × 70 000) $323 750
- fixed costs — it was assumed that all four activity levels are within the relevant range and therefore total fixed costs do not vary.

In the Pandion example total fixed costs and total variable costs were used for simplicity's sake to illustrate flexible budgeting concepts. Realistically, there are individual variable expenses and individual fixed expenses.

Each individual variable expense is treated the same as total variable expenses, that is, the cost per activity unit for the particular variable cost would be calculated and then multiplied by the number of activity units at each desired level.

Each individual fixed expense would be treated the same as total fixed expenses, that is, the particular fixed cost amount would remain the same regardless of the level of activity, provided the activity level selected remained within the relevant range.

Self-test problem 8.3

Refer to Self-test problems 8.1 and 8.2.

Required
Prepare a flexible budget at 190 000, 200 000 and 210 000 unit levels of activity. Show details for each individual cost item.

You should now be able to do Questions 8.2 to 8.5

Flexible budget analysis

Pandion Trophies Ltd is now in a position to better analyse the variances between actual and master budget. Below is a more detailed performance report for Pandion.

It can be seen that the variances from budget shown in the recast performance report (on page 167) can be broken down further. The detailed analysis allows management to more closely monitor performance and helps to pinpoint potential problem areas within the organisation.

Be aware that the illustration shown here is simplistic. Most managers will want even more detail and may want to see variable and fixed expenses itemised expense by expense.

Pandion Trophies Ltd

Detailed performance report for the year ended 30 June

	Master budget	Activity volume variance	Flexible budget for actual volume achieved	Flexible budget variance	Actual results
	Units	Units	Units	Units	Units
Trophies sold	80 000	5 000 *U*	75 000	—	75 000
	$	$	$	$	$
Sales	500 000	31 250 *U*	468 750	18 750 *U*	450 000
less **Variable costs**	370 000	23 125 *F*	346 875	6 875 *F*	340 000
Contribution margin	130 000	8 125 *U*	121 875	11 875 *U*	110 000
less **Fixed costs**	75 000	—	75 000	3 050 *U*	78 050
Net profit	55 000	8 125 *U*	46 875	14 925 *U*	31 950

$8125 *U*	$14 925 *U*
Total volume variances	Total flexible budget variances

$23 050
Static budget variance

Activity volume variance

The detailed performance report above shows the portion of each static budget variance which is caused by the fact that the actual volume achieved did not equal the desired volume on which the master budget was based.

In Pandion's case, the volume level is measured by number of units sold. Other organisations may base their budget on the volume of some other activity, for example, an accounting firm may use professional hours; a manufacturing organisation may use machine hours; and an educational institution may use student contact hours.

Note that the total budgeted fixed costs were the same at both levels. The volume variances for sales and variable costs were caused only by the difference in the volume levels because budgeted fixed cost per unit does not differ between activity levels within the relevant range.

Flexible budget variances

A comparison can now be made at the actual level achieved of 75 000 trophies. Flexible budget variances are due to differences between budget and actual sales prices, variable costs per unit incurred, and total fixed costs incurred.

Self-test problem 8.4

Refer to Self-test problems 8.1 and 8.3. The actual results for Anshar Manufacturing were:

	$
Sales (210 000 pens)	415 000
Variable costs	
Direct materials	150 000
Direct labour	48 600
Factory overhead	35 000
Selling	25 000
Administration and finance	10 000
Fixed costs	
Factory overhead	40 000
Selling	7 000
Administration and financial	22 000

Required
Prepare a detailed performance report. Use Pandion's detailed performance report as a guide, but list each expense, item by item.

You should now be able to do Questions 8.6 to 8.9

Checklist

Before finalising this chapter, complete the checklist below. This will identify whether you have an understanding of the important parts of the chapter.

Can you do the following?

- ☐ Identify and calculate contribution margin
- ☐ State the flexible budget formula
- ☐ Prepare flexible budgets for service operations
- ☐ Prepare flexible budgets for manufacturing organisations
- ☐ Identify static budget variances, activity volume variances and flexible budget variances

Questions

8.1 Yarillo Industries prepared the following static factory overhead budget for the coming year:

	$
Variable overhead	
Indirect labour	540 000
Supplies	734 400
Fixed overhead	
Supervision	388 800
Light and power	324 000
Depreciation	604 800
	2 592 000

The budgeted activity level is 318 600 machine hours. What is the flexible budget equation?

8.2 Flaming Foliage Sky Tours is a small sightseeing tour company in Western Australia. The firm specialises in aerial tours. Until recently, the company had not had an accounting department. Routine bookkeeping tasks had been handled by a person who had little formal training in accounting. As the business began to grow, however, the owner recognised the need for more formal accounting procedures. Jacqueline Frost has recently been hired as the new accountant and she will have authority to hire an assistant. During her first week on the job, Jacqueline was given the performance report shown below. The report was prepared by Red Leif, the company's manager of aircraft operations.

Flaming Foliage Sky Tours

Performance report for the month ended 30 September

	Actual	Static budget	Variance
Activity level			
Air km	32 000	35 000	3 000 *U*
	$	$	$
Passenger revenue	112 000	122 500	10 500 *U*
less **Variable expenses**			
Fuel	17 000	17 500	500 *F*
Aircraft maintenance	23 500	26 250	2 750 *F*
Flight crew salaries	13 100	14 000	900 *F*
Selling and administrative	24 900	28 000	3 100 *F*
Total variable expenses	78 500	85 750	7 250 *F*

(financial statement continued on next page)

(continued from previous page)

	Actual $	Static budget $	Variance $
Contribution margin	33 500	36 750	3 250 *U*
less **Fixed expenses**			
Depreciation on aircraft	2 900	2 900	—
Landing fees	1 000	900	100 *U*
Supervisory salaries	8 600	9 000	400 *F*
Selling and administrative	12 400	11 000	1 400 *U*
Total fixed expenses	24 900	23 800	1 100 *U*
Net profit	8 600	12 950	4 350 *U*

Required

Prepare a columnar flexible budget for Flaming Foliage Sky Tours' revenue and expenses, based on the following activity levels: 32 000 air kilometres, 35 000 air kilometres and 38 000 air kilometres.[1]

8.3 Amida Products is a manufacturing organisation. Amida's management would like a picture of the effect on profits of different activity levels. You are provided with the following details:

- Direct materials are $50 per unit.
- Direct labour costs $15 per hour. Each unit takes two hours to make.
- *Factory overhead:* Factory rent — $5000 per month; indirect labour — $7 000 per month, plus 10 cents per unit; labour on-costs are 20% of total labour costs; indirect material is $1 per unit; power, light and telephone are $2800 per month, plus 50 cents per unit; depreciation of factory plant is $72 000 per annum.
- Selling, administration and financial expenses (all fixed) are $480 000 per annum.
- There are no opening or closing stocks.
- Average selling price of Amida's products is $96.

Required

Prepare a flexible budget revenue statement for one month at sales levels of 100 000, 110 000 and 120 000 units per month.

8.4 Prepare a flexible budget for the production department from the following information:

	$
Fixed costs	
Depreciation	8 000
Supervision	16 000
Variable costs	
Indirect materials	8 000
Light and power	4 000
General expenses	5 000
Stores	3 000
Repairs	10 000

The above figures are for 100% capacity at which 10 000 units are produced. The budget is to be for 80%, 90% and 100% of capacity.

8.5 Checkem and Tickit are a firm of accountants specialising in auditing. They provide you, a junior partner, with the following data for the coming year ending 30 June:

- Estimated number of professional hours — 10 500. The charge out rate is $85 per professional hour.

Costs	
Partners' salaries (all fixed)	$420 000 pa
Support labour	Fixed — $105 000 pa Variable — $10 per professional hour
Photocopying (variable)	$0.25 per professional hour
Phones/faxes	Fixed — $5250 pa Variable — $0.50 per professional hour
Stationery (variable)	$1 per professional hour
Rent	$31 200 pa
Depreciation	$15 000 pa

Required

Prepare a flexible budget revenue statement at 10 000, 10 500 and 11 000 professional hours.

8.6 Refer to Question 8.2.

Required

(a) Prepare a detailed performance report which will show activity volume variances and flexible budget variances, item by item.

(b) In spite of several favourable variances in the original report, the company's September net income was only about two-thirds of the expected level. Why?

(c) Write a brief memo to the manager of aircraft operations explaining why the original variance report is misleading.[2]

8.7 Refer to Question 8.3. Amida Products' actual results for the budgeted month were:

- Units sold   95 000

	$
Sales	9 100 000
Variable expenses	
Direct materials	4 500 000
Direct labour	2 950 000
Indirect labour	9 000
Labour on-costs	600 000
Indirect material	90 000
Power, light and telephone	47 500
Fixed expenses	
Factory rent	5 100
Indirect labour	7 500
Labour on-costs	1 500
Power, light and telephone	2 500
Depreciation	6 000
Selling, administration and financial	42 000

- Amida set its master budget at the 100 000 activity level.

Required

Prepare a performance report which shows activity volume variances and flexible budget variances for the month.

8.8 Shamash Repairs had a small fire in its office. Several records were partly destroyed. The following budget information relevant to factory overhead information was salvaged.

	Amount per machine hour	Activity level (machine hours) 2 000	Activity level (machine hours) 3 000	Activity level (machine hours) 4 000
Variable factory overhead				
Indirect materials	$7	**(a)**	$21 000	**(b)**
Indirect labour	$5	$10 000	**(c)**	**(d)**
Power	$2	**(e)**	**(f)**	$8 000
Fixed factory overhead				
Depreciation on equipment		$25 000	**(g)**	**(h)**
Factory rent		**(i)**	$20 000	**(j)**
Supervision		**(k)**	**(l)**	$32 000

Required

Find the missing amounts identified by the letter **(a)** to **(l)** inclusive.

8.9 Statewide Realty provides you with the following performance report:

Statewide Realty

Performance report for the year ended 31 December

	Master budget $	Actual results $	Variances $
Total commissions received and other income	750 000	865 000	115 000 *F*
Commissions paid (all variable)	300 000	350 000	50 000 *U*
Motor vehicle expenses — fixed	6 500	7 000	500 *U*
Motor vehicle expenses — variable	6 500	7 200	700 *U*
Advertising — fixed	10 000	11 500	1 500 *U*
Advertising — variable	21 500	25 000	3 500 *U*
Office expenses (all fixed)	190 000	200 400	10 400 *U*
Total expenses	534 500	601 100	66 600 *U*
Net profit	215 500	263 900	48 400

Required

Recast the performance report so that it shows flexible budget variances. Budgeted variable expenses are based on a percentage of total revenue.

Endnotes

1 Adapted from Hilton, R. *Managerial Accounting*, 2nd edn, New York, USA: McGraw-Hill Book Company, 1994
2 Hilton

Solutions to self-test problems

Chapter 1

Self-test 1.1

Lanitza Holdings: Farm Machinery Division

Personnel department: Budget for the year ended 30 June

		$
Salaries	($154 000 × 1.05)	161 700
Stationery	($3520 × 1.03)	3 626
Telephone	($7000 × 0.96)	6 720
Electricity	($7680 × 1.02)	7 834
Office rent		18 000
Depreciation	[$6000 + 10% ($5000 − $4000)]	6 100
		203 980

Self-test 1.2

Big 'n Beefy Butchery

Performance report for the month of May

	Budget $	Actual $	Variances $	
Sales	40 000	41 500	1 500	F
less Cost of goods sold	25 000	24 000	1 000	F
Gross profit	15 000	17 500	2 500	F
Marketing expenses	1 000	1 200	200	U
Administration expenses	750	850	100	U
Financial expenses	500	450	50	F
Operating expenses	2 250	2 500	250	U
Net profit	12 750	15 000	2 250	F

Self-test 1.3

(a) False   (b) True   (c) False   (d) False   (e) True

Self-test 1.4

(a) Variable	(b) Fixed	(c) Variable
(d) Variable	(e) Fixed	(f) Variable

Self-test 1.5

1 (d)   2 (b)   3 (c)   4 (a)   5 (a)

Chapter 2

Self-test 2.1

1 (a)   2 (d)   3 (b)   4 (c)

Self-test 2.2

Halls Hardware: Gardening section

Sales budget for the year ending 30 June

Garden implement	Sales volume Units	Sales price $	Sales $
Spades	4 000	50	200 000
Forks	2 500	40	100 000
Hoes	2 000	30	60 000
			360 000

Self-test 2.3

- Present sales prices per litre:

Type of perfume	
Venus	$1 440 000/3600 = $400
Romantic Holiday	$1 750 000/5000 = $350
Balmy Breezes	$1 600 000/8000 = $200

- New selling prices per litre:

Type of perfume	
Venus	$400 × 0.94 = $376
Romantic Holiday	$350 × 0.94 = $329
Balmy Breezes	$200 × 1.1 = $220

- Anticipated sales volume in litres:

Type of perfume	
Venus	unchanged = 3600
Romantic Holiday	5000 × 1.02 = 5100
Balmy Breezes	8000 × 0.95 = 7600

Romanesque Fragrances Ltd

Sales budget for the year ending 30 June

Type of perfume	Sales volume Litres	Sales price $	Sales $
Venus	3 600	376	1 353 600
Romantic Holiday	5 100	329	1 677 900
Balmy Breezes	7 600	220	1 672 000
			4 703 500

Self-test 2.4

Electronics Inc.

Sales budget for the quarter ending 30 September

	July	August	September	Total for the quarter
Model SX3				
Sales volume	150	120	130	400
Selling price	$450	$450	$465	
Sales	$67 500	$54 000	$60 450	$181 950
Model TX5				
Sales volume	160	135	140	435
Selling price	$300	$310	$310	
Sales	$48 000	$41 850	$43 400	$133 250
Total sales	$115 500	$95 850	$103 850	$315 200

Self-test 2.5

The Mower Specialists

Sales budget for the quarter ending ...

	Month 1	Month 2	Month 3	Total for the quarter
Ballarat				
Two stroke				
Sales volume	15	18	19	52
Selling price	$450	$450	$475	
Sales	$6 750	$8 100	$9 025	$23 875
Four stroke				
Sales volume	10	12	16	38
Selling price	$600	$630	$630	
Sales	$6 000	$7 560	$10 080	$23 640
Ballarat sales	$12 750	$15 660	$19 105	$47 515
Bendigo				
Two stroke				
Sales volume	11	14	14	39
Selling price	$450	$450	$475	
Sales	$4 950	$6 300	$6 650	$17 900
Four stroke				
Sales volume	8	9	12	29
Selling price	$600	$630	$630	
Sales	$4 800	$5 670	$7 560	$18 030
Bendigo sales	$9 750	$11 970	$14 210	$35 930
Total sales	$22 500	$27 630	$33 315	$83 445

Self-test 2.6

- Anticipated client hours for next year:

Increase in market share	$3/22 \times 100 = 13.6364\%$
Estimated client hours	$15\,000 \times 1.136364\% = 17\,045$
Desired hourly rate	$\$85 \times 1.08 = \$91.80$

Manners and Fitzloon

Fees income budget for the year ending 30 June

Estimated client hours	17 045
Estimated hourly charge	$91.80
Fees income	$1 564 731

Self-test 2.7

(a) Fees income budget for the year:

- Hours of operation pa:

$$6 \times 1650 = 9900$$

- Time spent on each type of shampoo:

Super	30% × 9900 = 2970
Standard	50% × 9900 = 4950
Quick	20% × 9900 = 1980

- Number of each type of shampoo for year:

Super	2970/4 = 743
Standard	4950/3 = 1650
Quick	1980/2 = 990

- Cost of each type of shampoo:

Super	4 × $40 = $160
Standard	3 × $40 = $120
Quick	2 × $40 = $ 80

Brita Carpet Cleaning Services

Fees income budget for the year ending 30 June

Type of shampoo	Number of jobs	Price $	Fees $
Super	743	160	118 880
Standard	1 650	120	198 000
Quick	990	80	79 200
			396 080

(b) Fees income budget for the quarter:

- Number of shampoos per month:

Type	April	May	June
Super	(8% × 743) 59	(10% × 743) 74	(9% × 743) 67
Standard	(8% × 1650) 132	(10% × 1650) 165	(9% × 1650) 149
Quick	(8% × 990) 79	(10% × 990) 99	(9% × 990) 89

Brita Carpet Cleaning Services

Fees income budget for **the quarter ending 30 June**

	April	May	June	Total for the quarter
Super Shampoo				
Number of jobs	59	74	67	200
Price	$160	$160	$160	$160
Fees income	$9 440	$11 840	$10 720	$32 000
Standard Shampoo				
Number of jobs	132	165	149	446
Price	$120	$120	$120	$120
Fees income	$15 840	$19 800	$17 880	$53 520
Quick Shampoo				
Number of jobs	79	99	89	267
Price	$80	$80	$80	$80
Fees income	$6 320	$7 920	$7 120	$21 360
Total fees income	$31 600	$39 560	$35 720	$106 880

Chapter 3

Self-test 3.1

- Cost of sales:

January	$100 000
February	$120 000
March	$80 000
April	$110 000

- Opening stock:

January	$100 000 × 90%	=	$90 000
February	$120 000 × 90%	=	$108 000
March	$80 000 × 90%	=	$72 000
April	$110 000 × 90%	=	$99 000

Oarsome Rowing Equipment Co.

Purchases budget for the 3 months ending 31 March

	January $	February $	March $	Quarter $
Cost of sales	100 000	120 000	80 000	300 000
add Closing stock	108 000	72 000	99 000	99 000
Total requirements	208 000	192 000	179 000	399 000
less Opening stock	90 000	108 000	72 000	90 000
Purchases	118 000	84 000	107 000	309 000

Self-test 3.2

Framm Company

Purchases budget for the quarter 30 June

	April	May	June	Quarter
Sales (units)	3 000	3 300	3 200	9 500
add Ending Inventory (units)	1 650	1 600	1 500	1 500
Total requirements (units)	4 650	4 900	4 700	11 000
less Beginning inventory (units)	1 500	1 650	1 600	1 500
Purchases (in units)	3 150	3 250	3 100	9 500
Cost per unit	× $150	× $150	× $150	× $150
Cost of purchases	$472 500	$487 500	$465 000	$1 425 000

Self-test 3.3

Romanesque Fragrances Ltd

Purchases budget for the year ending 30 June

	Venus $	Romantic Holiday $	Balmy Breezes $	Total $
Cost of sales	676 800	838 950	836 000	2 351 750
add Ending inventory	59 558	73 828	73 568	206 954
Total requirements	736 358	912 778	909 568	2 558 704
less Beginning inventory	54 144	67 116	66 880	188 140
Purchases	682 214	845 662	842 688	2 370 564

Self-test 3.4

Oarsome Rowing Equipment Co.

Cost of goods sold budget for the 3 months ending 31 March

	January $	February $	March $	Quarter $
Opening stock	90 000	108 000	72 000	90 000
Purchases	118 000	84 000	107 000	309 000
Goods available for sale	208 000	192 000	179 000	399 000
less Closing stock	108 000	72 000	99 000	99 000
Cost of goods sold	100 000	120 000	80 000	300 000

Self-test 3.5

Expense	January	February	March
Sales representatives' salaries	$72 000/12 = $6 000	$6 000	$6 000
Cartage out	5% × $150 000 = $7 500	5% × $180 000 = $9 000	5% × $120 000 = $6 000
Advertising	3% × $150 000 = $4 500	3% × $180 000 = $5 400	3% × $120 000 = $3 600

Oarsome Rowing Equipment Co.

Marketing expenses budget for the 3 months ending 31 March

	January $	February $	March $	Quarter $
Sales representatives' salaries	6 000	6 000	6 000	18 000
Cartage out	7 500	9 000	6 000	22 500
Advertising	4 500	5 400	3 600	13 500
Total marketing expenses	18 000	20 400	15 600	54 000

Self-test 3.6

General salaries and wages	$144 000/12	= $12 000 per month
Audit fees	$2 400/12	= $200 per month
Salary on-costs	15% × ($6000 + $12 000)	= $2700 per month
Rent	$43 200/12	= $3600 per month
Depreciation	$27 600/12	= $2300 per month
Telephone	$1800/12	= $150 per month
Stationery	$1800/12	= $150 per month

Oarsome Rowing Equipment Co.

**Administration expenses budget
for the 3 months ending 31 March**

	January $	February $	March $	Quarter $
General salaries and wages	12 000	12 000	12 000	36 000
Audit fees	200	200	200	600
Salary on-costs	2 700	2 700	2 700	8 100
Rent	3 600	3 600	3 600	10 800
Depreciation	2 300	2 300	2 300	6 900
Telephone	150	150	150	450
Stationery	150	150	150	450
Total administration expenses	21 100	21 100	21 100	63 300

Self-test 3.7

Oarsome Rowing Equipment Co.

Financial expenses budget for the 3 months ending 31 March

	January $	February $	March $	Quarter $
Interest on loan	830	820	810	2 460
Bank charges etc	60	60	60	180
Total financial expenses	890	880	870	2 640

Self-test 3.8

Oarsome Rowing Equipment Co.

**Budgeted revenue statement
for the 3 months ending 31 March**

	January $	February $	March $	Quarter $
Sales	150 000	180 000	120 000	450 000
less Cost of goods sold	100 000	120 000	80 000	300 000
Gross profit	50 000	60 000	40 000	150 000
less Operating expenses				
Marketing expenses	18 000	20 400	15 600	54 000
Administration expenses	21 100	21 100	21 100	63 300
Financial expenses	890	880	870	2 640
Total operating expenses	39 990	42 380	37 570	119 940
Net profit	10 010	17 620	2 430	30 060

(Self-test solutions continue next page)

Self-test 3.9

Oarsome Rowing Equipment Co.

**Budgeted revenue statement
for the 3 months ending 31 March**

	January $	February $	March $	Quarter $
Sales	150 000	180 000	120 000	450 000
less **Cost of goods sold**				
Opening stock	90 000	108 000	72 000	90 000
Purchases	118 000	84 000	107 000	309 000
Goods available for sale	208 000	192 000	179 000	399 000
less Closing stock	108 000	72 000	99 000	99 000
Cost of goods sold	100 000	120 000	80 000	300 000
Gross profit	50 000	60 000	40 000	150 000
less **Operating expenses**				
Marketing expenses				
Sales representatives' salaries	6 000	6 000	6 000	18 000
Cartage out	7 500	9 000	6 000	22 500
Advertising	4 500	5 400	3 600	13 500
Total marketing expenses	18 000	20 400	15 600	54 000
Administration expenses				
General salaries and wages	12 000	12 000	12 000	36 000
Audit fees	200	200	200	600
Salary on-costs	2 700	2 700	2 700	8 100
Rent	3 600	3 600	3 600	10 800
Depreciation	2 300	2 300	2 300	6 900
Telephone	150	150	150	450
Stationery	150	150	150	450
Total administration expenses	21 100	21 100	21 100	63 300
Financial expenses				
Interest on loan	830	820	810	2 460
Bank charges etc	60	60	60	180
Total financial expenses	890	880	870	2 640
Total operating expenses	39 990	42 380	37 570	119 940
Net profit	10 010	17 620	2 430	30 060

Self-test 3.10

Manners and Fitzloon

**Professional and support labour budget
for the quarter ending ...**

	Month 1	Month 2	Month 3	Quarter
Professional labour hours	765	810	792	2 367
Average cost per hour	× $55	× $55	× $55	× $55
Professional labour cost	$42 075	$44 550	$43560	$130 185
Support labour hours	935	990	968	2 893
Average cost per hour	× $30	× $30	× $31.50	
Support labour cost	$28 050	$29 700	$30492	$88 242
Total professional and support labour	$70 125	$74 250	$74 052	$218 427

Self-test 3.11

H. Bennett

Garden and landscape supplies usage budget for the year ending ...

	$
Beginning inventory	5 100
Purchases	21 300
	26 400
less Ending inventory	5 500
Supplies used	20 900

Chapter 4

Self-test 4.1

St. Jude's

Cash receipts budget for the quarter ending 31 March

	January $	February $	March $	Quarter $
Fees received	14 800	13 300	14 700	42 800
Sale of instruments	1 600	1 600	2 100	5 300
Total cash receipts	16 400	14 900	16 800	48 100

Self-test 4.2

M. Street

Cash payments budget for the quarter ending 30 June

	April $	May $	June $	Quarter $
Advertising	170	160	200	530
Bank charges etc	25	25	25	75
Cleaning	190	200	190	580
Hairdressers' wages	5 200	5 250	5 300	15 750
Hairdressing implements				
— replacements		180		180
Purchases				
— hairdressing materials	800	850	820	2 470
Interest on loan	510	440	360	1 310
Light and power	780			780
Office staff wages	1 750	1 750	1 750	5 250
Rent	2 160	2 160	2 400	6 720
Stationery and postage			120	120
Insurances		1 500		1 500
Salon equipment	1 500			1 500
Total cash payments	13 085	12 515	11 165	36 765

Self-test 4.3

M. Street

Cash budget for the quarter ending 30 June

	April $	May $	June $
Opening balance	1 210	(2 035)	(1 290)
add Receipts	9 840	13 260	14 780
Cash available for needs	11 050	11 225	13 490
less Payments	13 085	12 515	11 165
Closing balance	(2 035)	(1 290)	2 325

Self-test 4.4

(a) Cash receipts budget:

- Calculate cash and credit sales:

	Apr. $	May $	Jun. $	Jul. $	Aug. $	Sept. $
Cash sales (70%)	36 400	54 600	59 150	45 500	59 150	63 700
Credit sales (30%)	15 600	23 400	25 350	19 500	25 350	27 300
	52 000	78 000	84 500	65 000	84 500	91 000

Fellini Fashions

Schedule of collections from accounts receivable for the quarter ending 30 September

		Month received		
Month of sale	$	July $	August $	September $
April	15 600	(10%) 1 560		
May	23 400	(40%) 9 360	(10%) 2 340	
June	25 350	(50%) 12 675	(40%) 10 140	(10%) 2 535
July	19 500		(50%) 9 750	(40%) 7 800
August	25 350			(50%) 12 675
Total collections		23 595	22 230	23 010

Fellini Fashions

Cash receipts budget for the quarter ending 30 September

	July $	August $	September $	Quarter $
Cash sales	45 500	59 150	63 700	168 350
Collections from accounts receivable	23 595	22 230	23 010	68 835
Total cash receipts	69 095	81 380	86 710	237 185

(b) Accounts receivable balance as at 30 September:

		$
From July sales	(10% × $19 500)	1 950
From August sales	(50% × $25 350)	12 675
From September sales		27 300
		41 925

Self-test 4.5

- Calculate cash and credit sales:

	Aug. $	Sept. $	Oct. $	Nov. $	Dec. $
Cash sales (45%)	32 400	29 700	40 500	48 600	43 200
Credit sales (55%)	39 600	36 300	49 500	59 400	52 800
	72 000	66 000	90 000	108 000	96 000

Nuada Enterprises

Schedule of collections from accounts receivable for the quarter ending 31 December

		Month of receipt		
Month of sale	Workings	Oct. $	Nov. $	Dec. $
August	25% × $39 600	9 900		
September	30% × $36 300	10 890		
	25% × $36 300		9 075	
October	40% × $49 500 × 95%	18 810		
	30% × $49 500		14 850	
	25% × $49 500			12 375
November	40% × $59 400 × 95%		22 572	
	30% × $59 400			17 820
December	40% × $52 800 × 95%			20 064
Total collections		39 600	46 497	50 259

Self-test 4.6

Potamid's Pool Playthings

Purchases budget for the 2 months ending 30 April

		March $		April $
Sales (at cost)	55/100 × $77 500	42 625	55/100 × $68 700	37 785
Closing inventory		46 717	$44 660 + 20% × $41 250	52 910
Total needs		89 342		90 695
Opening inventory		63 000	$37 785 + 20% × $44 660	46 717
Purchases		26 342		43 978

Potamid's Pool Playthings

Schedule of payments for purchases for the 2 months ending 30 April

		Month of receipt	
Month of purchase	**Workings**	**March $**	**April $**
January	10% × $47 500	4 750	
February	50% × $50 500	25 250	
	10% × $50 500		5 050
March	40% × $26 342 × 95%	10 010	
	50% × $26 342		13 171
April	40% × $43 978 × 95%		16 712
Total payments		40 010	34 933

Self-test 4.7

Parvati Products

Schedule of collections from accounts receivable for the quarter ending 31 December

		Month received		
Month of sale	$	October $	November $	December $
August	14 700	(20%) 2 940		
September	8 100	(80%) 6 480	(20%) 1 620	
October	13 200		(80%) 10 560	(20%) 2 640
November	15 300			(80%) 12 240
Total collections		9 420	12 180	14 880

Parvati Products

Cash budget for the 3 months ending 31 December

	October $	November $	December $
Beginning cash balance — surplus/(deficiency)	2 550	14 280	9 135
Receipts			
Cash sales	22 800	14 340	17 490
Collections from accounts receivable	9 420	12 180	14 880
Total receipts	32 220	26 520	32 370
Cash available for needs	34 770	40 800	41 505
Payments			
Cash purchases	5 940	9 450	9 180
Accounts payable	7 650	15 315	6 525
Wages	6 900	6 900	6 900
Insurance			4 500
Total payments	20 490	31 665	27 105
Closing cash balance — surplus/(deficiency)	14 280	9 135	14 400

Self-test 4.8

(a) 25 000	(b) 35 750	(c) 214 250	(d) 81 250	(e) 26 000
(f) 25 000	(g) 235 750	(h) 10 250	(i) 5 000	(j) (5 000)
(k) (50)	(l) 5 000	(m) 25 000		

Chapter 5

Self-test 5.1

Ammon Artefacts

Budgeted revenue statement
for the 3 months ending 30 September

	July $	August $	September $	Quarter $
Sales	22 000	23 000	23 500	68 500
less **Cost of goods sold**				
Opening stock	22 000	23 000	23 500	22 000
Purchases	16 200	16 960	17 490	50 650
Goods available for sale	38 200	39 960	40 990	72 650
less Closing stock	23 000	23 500	24 400	24 400
Cost of goods sold	15 200	16 460	16 590	48 250
Gross profit	6 800	6 540	6 910	20 250
less **Operating expenses**				
Marketing expenses				
Sales commission	1 100	1 150	1 175	3 425
Depreciation — shop fixtures	600	600	600	1 800
Total marketing expenses	1 700	1 750	1 775	5 225
Administration expenses				
Rent	1 600	1 600	1 600	4 800
Telephone and stationery	175	175	175	525
Depreciation:				
Motor vehicles	500	500	500	1 500
Office equipment	190	190	190	570
Total administration expenses	2 465	2 465	2 465	7 395
Financial expenses				
Bad debts	220	230	235	685
Bank charges etc	60	60	60	180
Total financial expenses	280	290	295	865
Total operating expenses	4 445	4 505	4 535	13 485
Net profit	2 355	2 035	2 375	6 765

Self-test 5.2

A. Green and Associates

Budgeted revenue statement for the year ending 30 June

	$	$	$
Fees income			648 648
less **Operating expenses**			484 081
Draughting		261 881	
Contract draught person	26 754		
Draught persons' salaries	228 585		
Printing of plans	6 542		
Marketing		12 973	
Advertising	12 973		
Administration		187 513	
Accounting fees	6 983		
Motor vehicle expenses	7 350		
Office salaries	102 900		
Rent	26 400		
Subscriptions to professional association	1 890		
Telephone and stationery	4 190		
Travelling	37 800		
Financial		21 714	
Bad debts	6 486		
Bank charges etc	2 478		
Interest expense	12 750		
Net profit			164 567

Self-test 5.3

- Sales:

Month		Credit $		Cash $	Total $
January	40% × $25 000		60% × $25 000 × 95%		
		10 000		14 250	24 250
February	40% × $30 000		60% × $30 000 × 95%		
		12 000		17 100	29 100
March	40% × $35 000		60% × $35 000 × 95%		
		14 000		19 950	33 950
		36 000		51 300	87 300

- Purchases:

		$
January	75% × $25 000	18 750
February	75% × $30 000	22 500
March	75% × $35 000	26 250
		67 500

- Discount received:

		$
January	80% × $18 750 × 2%	300
February	80% × $22 500 × 2%	360
March	80% × $26 250 × 2%	420
		1 080

- Bad debts:

		$
January	5% × $10 000	500
February	5% × $12 000	600
March	5% × $14 000	700
		1 800

- Discount allowed:

		$
January	50% × $10 000 × 3%	150
February	50% × $12 000 × 3%	180
March	50% × $14 000 × 3%	210
		540

Gaea Gallery

Budgeted revenue statement for the quarter ending 31 March

	$	$	$
Sales			87 300
less **Cost of goods sold**			64 500
Opening inventory		12 000	
Purchases		67 500	
Goods available for sale		79 500	
less Closing inventory		15 000	
Gross profit			22 800
Other operating income			1 080
Discount received		1 080	
Operating income			23 880
less **Operating expenses**			11 340
Marketing		3 000	
Administration		6 000	
Financial		2 340	
Bad debts	1 800		
Discount allowed	540		
Net profit			12 540

Self-test 5.4

- Collections from accounts receivable:

Month of sale	Workings	Month of receipt		
		January $	February $	March $
Balance 31/12	Given	6 750	2 400	
January	50% × $10 000 × 97%	4 850		
	30% × $10 000		3 000	
	15% × $10 000			1 500
February	50% × $12 000 × 97%		5 820	
	30% × $12 000			3 600
March	50% × $14 000 × 97%			6 790
Total collections		11 600	11 220	11 890

- Payments to accounts payable:

Month of purchase	Workings	Month of payment		
		January $	February $	March $
December	From balance sheet	6 000		
January	80% × $18 750 × 98%	14 700		
	20% × $18 750		3 750	
February	80% × $22 500 × 98%		17 640	
	20% × $22 500			4 500
March	80% × $26 250 × 98%			20 580
Total		20 700	21 390	25 080

- Balance of accounts receivable:

		$
February sales	(15% × $12 000)	1 800
March sales	(45% × $14 000)	6 300
		8 100

- Balance of accounts payable:

March purchases	(20% × $26 250)	$5250

- Balance of mortgage:

$$\$12\,000 - \$3000 = \$9000$$

- Balance of accumulated depreciation

$$3 \times \$375 + \$12\,500 = \$13\,625$$

- Expenses paid each month:

Marketing		$1 000
Administration	$2000 − $375	$1 625

Gaea Gallery

Cash budget for the 3 months ending 31 March

	January $	February $	March $
Beginning cash balance — surplus	5 000	7 525	8 830
Receipts			
Cash sales	14 250	17 100	19 950
Collections from accounts receivable	11 600	11 220	11 890
Total receipts	25 850	28 320	31 840
Cash available for needs	30 850	35 845	40 670
Payments			
Accounts payable	20 700	21 390	25 080
Marketing expenses	1 000	1 000	1 000
Administration expenses	1 625	1 625	1 625
Mortgage repayment		3 000	
Total payments	23 325	27 015	27 705
Closing cash balance — surplus	7 525	8 830	12 965

Gaea Gallery

Budgeted balance sheet as at 31 March

	$	$
Proprietor's funds		
Capital 1 January		25 650
add Net profit		12 540
Total proprietor's funds		38 190
Represented by:		
Current assets		36 065
Bank	12 965	
Accounts receivable	8 100	
Inventory	15 000	
Current liability		5 250
Accounts payable	5 250	
Working capital		30 815
Non-current assets		16 375
Equipment	30 000	
less Accumulated depreciation	13 625	
		47 190
less **Non-current liability**		9 000
Mortgage	9 000	
Net assets		38 190

Self-test 5.5

- Collections from customers:

	January $	February $	March $	Quarter $
Cash sales	14 250	17 100	19 950	51 300
Collections from accounts receivable	11 600	11 220	11 890	34 710
	25 850	28 320	31 840	86 010

- Payments to employees:

     $1000 per month × 3 months = $3000

- Payments to suppliers:

	January $	February $	March $	Quarter $
Payments to accounts payable	20 700	21 390	25 080	67 170
Marketing expense payments	1 000	1 000	1 000	3 000
Administration expense payments	1 625	1 625	1 625	4 875
	23 325	24 015	27 705	75 045
less Payments to employees	1 000	1 000	1 000	3 000
	22 325	23 015	26 705	72 045

Gaea Gallery

**Budgeted statement of cash flows
for the quarter ending 31 March**

	$	$
Cash flows from operating activities		
Inflows:		
Collections from customers		86 010
Outflows:		
Payments to employees	(3 000)	
Payments to suppliers	(72 045)	(75 045)
Net cash inflow from operating activities		10 965
Cash flows from investing activities		Nil
Cash flows from financing activities		
Repayment of mortgage	(3 000)	
Net cash outflow from financing activities		(3 000)
Net increase in cash held		7 965
Cash balance 1 January		5 000
Cash balance 31 March		12 965

Chapter 6

Self-test 6.1

(a) Product   (b) Period   (c) Period   (d) Period   (e) Product
(f) Product   (g) Period   (h) Period   (i) Product   (j) Product

Self-test 6.2

(a) Indirect   (b) Direct   (c) Indirect   (d) Indirect   (e) Direct
(f) Indirect   (g) Indirect   (h) Direct   (i) Direct   (j) Indirect

Self-test 6.3

Loreston Timeworks

**Production budget
for the quarter ending 31 March**

	Clocks
Sales	6 000
Ending inventory	550
Total clocks needed	6 550
less Ending inventory	400
Clocks to be produced	6 150

Self-test 6.4

Storf Industries

**Production budget
for the quarter ending 30 September**

	July	August	September	Total
Sales — units	2 450	2 220	2 485	7 155
add Ending inventory	2 030	1 990	2 250	2 250
Units needed	4 480	4 210	4 735	9 405
less Beginning inventory	2 230	2 030	1 990	2 230
Units to be produced	2 250	2 180	2 745	7 175

Storf Industries

**Direct materials usage budget
for the quarter ending 30 September**

	July	August	September	Total
Units to be produced	2 250	2 180	2 745	7 175
kg per unit	× 4	× 4	× 4	× 4
Direct materials needed for production — units	9 000	8 720	10 980	28 700
Cost per kg	× $3.60	× $3.60	× $3.60	× $3.60
Cost of direct materials needed for production	$32 400	$31 392	$39 528	$103 320

Self-test 6.5

Dagda Company

**Direct materials purchases budget
for the quarter ending 31 March**

	January	February	March	Total
Estimated production — units	7 400	8 900	8 300	24 600
Units of direct material required	× 3	× 3	× 3	× 3
Direct materials needed for production — units	22 200	26 700	24 900	73 800
add Closing stock	16 020	14 940	14 400*	14 400
Total direct material needed	38 220	41 640	39 300	88 200
less Opening stock	13 320	16 020	14 940	13 320
Direct material to be purchased — units	24 900	25 620	24 360	74 880
Cost per unit	$4	× $4	× $4	× $4
Cost of direct materials needed for production	$99 600	$102 480	$97 440	$299 520

* 8000 × 3 × 60%

Self-test 6.6

Samsara Productions

Direct labour budget
for the year ending 30 June

Annual production in units	(1 900 × 48)	91 200
Hours to produce one unit		× 5
Direct labour required *for production — hours*		456 000
Direct labour cost per hour		× $17.35
Direct labour cost		$7 911 600

Self-test 6.7

Renpet Industries

Factory overhead budget
for the year ending 30 June, Year 2

		$
Indirect labour	($96 300 × 1.1)	105 930
Indirect material	($39 100 × 1.15)	44 965
Cleaning	($35 500 × 1.05)	37 275
Light and power	($43 100 × 1.08)	46 548
Rent	($60 000 × 1.02)	61 200
Insurance	($34 400 × 1.06)	36 464
Repairs and maintenance	($39 900 × 1.05)	41 895
Depreciation	($30 000 × 1.05)	31 500
Miscellaneous	($28 600 × 1.12)	32 032
Total factory overhead		437 809

Self-test 6.8

(a) $437 809/9500 = $46.0852 per direct labour hour

(b) 780 × $46.0852 = $35 946

Self-test 6.9

A. Business

Factory overhead budget for the month ending 31 August

		$
Fixed overhead		12 000
Variable overhead	(7 500 × $1.75)	13 125
Total factory overhead		25 125

Self-test 6.10

- Cost per unit of finished product:

		$
Direct material	2 Litres @ $7 per Litre	14
Direct labour	0.5 hours @ $18 per hour	9
Factory overhead	0.5 hours @ $20 per hour	10
		33

Endorfin Concentrates

Ending inventory budget as at 30 November

		$
Finished goods	3000 units @ $33 per unit	99 000
Direct material	5000 Litres @ $7 per Litre	35 000
		134 000

Self-test 6.11

- Cost of production:

		$
Direct material	5000 × $22	110 000
Direct labour	5000 × $30	150 000
Factory overhead	5000 × $15	75 000
		335 000

Fravak Engineering

Cost of goods sold budget for the month ending 31 May

	$
Beginning inventory	35 000
Cost of production	335 000
Goods available for sale	370 000
less Ending inventory	40 200
Cost of goods sold	329 800

Self-test 6.12

- Valuation of production and inventories:

		$
Production		
April	3030 units @ $45 per unit	136 350
May	3660 units @ $50 per unit	183 000
June	3960 units @ $50 per unit	198 000
Inventories		
1 April	120 units @ $45 per unit	5 400
30 April	150 units @ $45 per unit	6 750
31 May	210 units @ $50 per unit	10 500
30 June	270 units @ $50 per unit	13 500

Yasna and Zorya

Cost of goods sold budget for the quarter ending 30 June

	April $	May $	June $	Total $
Beginning inventory	5 400	6 750	10 500	5 400
Cost of production	136 350	183 000	198 000	517 350
Goods available for sale	141 750	189 750	208 500	522 750
less Ending inventory	6 750	10 500	13 500	13 500
Cost of goods sold	135 000	179 250	195 000	509 250

Yasna and Zorya

Budgeted revenue statement for the quarter ending 30 June

	April $	May $	June $	Total $
Sales	225 000	288 000	312 000	825 000
less **Cost of goods sold**	135 000	179 250	195 000	509 250
Gross profit	90 000	108 750	117 000	315 750
less **Operating expenses**				
Marketing	14 400	16 200	17 400	48 000
Administration	18 000	20 250	21 750	60 000
Financial	3 600	4 050	4 350	12 000
Total operating expenses	36 000	40 500	43 500	120 000
Net profit/(loss)	54 000	68 250	73 500	195 750

Chapter 7

Self-test 7.1

• Partial organisation chart for Lanitza Holdings:

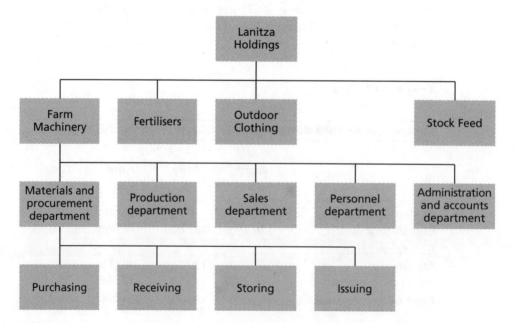

Self-test 7.2

(a) Revenue centre
(b) Profit centre
(c) Cost centre
(d) Investment centre
(e) Cost centre
(f) Revenue centre
(g) Profit centre
(h) Cost centre

Self-test 7.3

Lanitza Holdings: Farm Machinery division

Personnel department: Performance report for December

	Budget $	Actual $	Variance $
Salaries	14 553	15 100	547 *U*
Stationery	272	256	16 *F*
Telephone	504	478	26 *F*
Electricity	588	569	19 *F*
Office Rent	1 500	1 550	50 *U*
Depreciation	508	508	—
	17 925	18 461	536 *U*

Self-test 7.4

(a) Performance report showing percentage variance:

Lanitza Holdings: Farm Machinery division

Personnel department: Performance report for December

	Budget $	Actual $	Variance $	Variance %
Salaries	14 553	15 100	547 *U*	3.76 *U*
Stationery	272	256	16 *F*	5.88 *F*
Telephone	504	478	26 *F*	5.16 *F*
Electricity	588	569	19 *F*	3.23 *F*
Office Rent	1 500	1 550	50 *U*	3.33 *U*
Depreciation	508	508	—	—
	17 925	18 461	536 *U*	2.99 *U*

(b) Stationery and telephone need to be investigated.

Chapter 8

Self-test 8.1

Anshar Manufacturing

**Recast budgeted revenue statement
for the year ending 30 June**

	$	$
Sales (200 000 pens)		400 000
less **Variable expenses**		250 000
Direct materials	140 000	
Direct labour	48 000	
Factory overhead	32 000	
Selling	22 000	
Administration and financial	8 000	
Contribution margin		150 000
less **Fixed expenses**		71 000
Factory overhead	40 000	
Selling	6 000	
Administration and financial	25 000	
Net profit		79 000

Self-test 8.2

(a) Flexible budget equation:

Variable cost per pen sold =
$250 000/200 000 = $1.25

Total budgeted expenses = ($1.25 × number of pens sold)
+ $71 000

(b) Average budgeted price:

Average price per pen =
$400 000/200 000 = $2

Self-test 8.3

Anshar Manufacturing

Flexible budget for the year ending 30 June

	Per unit	190 000 $	200 000 $	210 000 $
		Activity level (pens sold)		
Sales	($2.00)	380 000	400 000	420 000
less **Variable costs**				
Direct materials	($0.70)	133 000	140 000	147 000
Direct labour	($0.24)	45 600	48 000	50 400
Factory overhead	($0.16)	30 400	32 000	33 600
Selling	($0.11)	20 900	22 000	23 100
Administration and Financial	($0.04)	7 600	8 000	8 400
Total variable costs	($1.25)	237 500	250 000	262 500
Contribution margin	($0.75)	142 500	150 000	157 500
less **Fixed costs**				
Factory overhead		40 000	40 000	40 000
Selling		6 000	6 000	6 000
Administration and financial		25 000	25 000	25 000
Total fixed costs		71 000	71 000	71 000
Net profit		71 500	79 000	86 500

Self-test 8.4

Anshar Manufacturing

Performance report for the year ended 30 June

	Master budget	Activity volume variance	Flexible budget	Flexible budget variance	Actual results
Pens sold	200 000	10 000 *F*	210 000	—	210 000
	$	$	$	$	$
Sales	400 000	20 000 *F*	420 000	5 000 *U*	415 000
less **Variable costs**					
Direct materials	140 000	7 000 *U*	147 000	3 000 *U*	150 000
Direct labour	48 000	2 400 *U*	50 400	1 800 *F*	48 600
Factory overhead	32 000	1 600 *U*	33 600	1 400 *U*	35 000
Selling	22 000	1 100 *U*	23 100	1 900 *U*	25 000
Administration and financial	8 000	400 *U*	8 400	1 600 *U*	10 000
Total variable expenses	250 000	12 500 *U*	262 500	6 100 *U*	268 600
Contribution margin	150 000	7 500 *F*	157 500	11 100 *U*	146 400
less **Fixed costs**					
Factory overhead	40 000	—	40 000	—	40 000
Selling	6 000	—	6 000	1 000 *U*	7 000
Administration and financial	25 000	—	25 000	3 000 *F*	22 000
Total fixed expenses	71 000	—	71 000	2 000 *F*	69 000
Net profit	79 000	7 500 *F*	86 500	9 100 *U*	77 400

Index